Free the Girl
A story about finding self-love

Maya Kiusalaas

Copyright © Maya Kiusalaas, 2017
Cover copyright © Max Kiusalaas, 2017
Photo copyright © Max Kiusalaas and listed artists, 2017
Illustration copyright © Inka Kiusalaas Kivinen and listed artists, 2017

All Rights Reserved.

No part of this publication may be reproduced, stored in a retrieval system, or transmitted in any form or by any means, electronic, mechanical, photocopying, recording or otherwise, with out the prior permission of the publishers.

Dedicated to:
My teenage self, but also to Adrian. With this book I am finally able to leave what I don't want behind and focus all my love on what I truly want in the future, which is a happy life with you, my Adrian!

Table of Contents

PROLOGUE	1
IT ALWAYS STARTS WITH A HOODIE	12
LIFE IS PISS	22
BEING YOURSELF	29
EMBARRASSMENT	35
THE FUCKING FORD	40
THINGS THAT HURT	48
WHAT IF PEOPLE ACTUALLY SEE (THE REAL) ME?	54
SO I AM NOT A FUCKING GYMNAST?	61
BIOLOGY CLASS IN YEAR EIGHT	67
IDEALS & OBSESSIONS	73
I AM NOT MYSELF	79
HELP!	86
THE LUNCH GROUP	96
THE BLACK SHEEP	102
LOOKING BACK	107
MOST OF THE HORROR I WILL SPARE YOU	112

WHAT IF MY FRIEND IS STRUGGLING?	122
THE UNIVERSE INSIDE OF US	132
GUT HEALTH	140
IT'S ALL ONE FUCKING PARTY	145
THE BOOK SHELF	151
COCKTAIL HOUR	155
I REMEMBER	164
SHOOT ME	173
MY CONCRETE MUM	179
PLEASE FIX ME	184
MY WORLD IS A COUCH	209
PIECE OF SHIT	215
WHAT AM I DOING WITH MY LIFE?	222
PSYCHOLOGY HOPPING	227
THERE IS NOTHING WRONG WITH ME!!!	235
THE SPIRAL	242
THE SOLUTIONS – NOT PROBLEMS	247
FEELING GOOD	254
VISION & GOALS	260
GRATITUDE	265

CRAZY IS PERFECT	273
TWO STEPS FORWARD AND ONE STEP BACK	282
CLICK	291
GO WITH THE INNER FLOW	295
THE MIND GAMES	299
PEOPLE ARE JUST PEOPLE, LIKE YOU	305
MAGIC	311
THE END, THE BEGINNING, WHATEVER YOU WANT IT TO BE	315
FOLLOW THE TRACE, BACK TO THE SOURCE…	322

PROLOGUE

To you, the beautiful reader of this book!

This is not a book of answers, it is a book of questions.

Not just any questions, important and interesting questions to **uncover who you really are**, get to know yourself more than you ever believed you could, and take you places in this world you mightn't even have dared to dream of.

This book is about exploring limitless possibilities and learning to see the world with an open mind. This book is for you who knows what it's like to feel like shit, and who is determined not to settle for that feeling. The questions inside are designed to get you to know yourself on a deeper level and uncover new truths about yourself.

As you have probably heard a million times; **you are unique** and this is so true. Every person will read this book and answer the questions differently. Why are you different to your friends, your family and the rest of the world? Because nobody on the planet is made out of the exact same combination of genes, DNA and social experiences. You are the only one who has been through the things that you have been through and experienced them your way. You are unique in the way you feel things, the way you see things. What your brain takes in is individual to you. Only you read what you read, see what you see, hear what you hear, learn what you learn, love what you love in the way that you love it.

So when it comes to the questions of who you are, you are the only person with the real answer.

Nobody can tell you what is true to you, you have to feel it.

As you read this book and learn, just also know that what you believe and the truth you hold in this moment can, and will change throughout your life. That is a good thing because it is what keeps creating you. I ask that whatever you learn here, continue to listen to the changes, be aware of new perceptions and grow with them. Keep discovering!

I wrote this book because as a teenager, I wasn't able to help myself. I hated who I was and I felt helpless, like I was a victim of my own life. I believed that I would have to live with eating disorders for the rest of my life and that I would never feel proud to be me. Living felt hard and I believed that it would always feel hard. That was before I started to really look to find and support my true inner values. Eventually, I started to value what was really interesting to me, from the inside and out. Now I believe that I have the knowledge and wisdom to heal.

From time to time this book might open up feelings of sadness, because of the bleeding wounds I used to hold onto. Sadness used to be what inspired me the most, which only brought me closer to sad places. Don't be afraid of the sadness, if you can relate to my wounds, please feel them with me. I do ask that even if you feel sad, you take inspiration from happiness, strength, freedom and growth. Focus on those feelings, the positive things that will take you closer to positive places.

I know it may be hard sometimes to focus on good things, but please, know that this comes from a person who believed that she could never, ever, love herself at all. Believe me when I say that you become what you focus on the most. So, focus on the really fucking good things! And when everything around you is shit, find inspiration to turn that shit into something good. Express it in writing, painting, turn it into music or use it as motivation to improve yourself. Move to passion.

Even though I had a fantastic mix of cool and kind friends, the best family and everything I needed to create an exciting life for myself, I didn't know how to love myself. I constantly felt like I didn't belong, that I was worthless. I compared myself to the girls around me and used that comparison to be unhappy.

Through helping my own teenage self in this book, I hope that I can be the light at the end of more tunnels, maybe the light at the end of yours. Through sharing my mistakes and what I have learned, I trust that I can be an inspiration for those who might be stuck in the same dark and unfulfilled places that I once was.

This book is everything I wished I knew then.

Would I change anything about the journey I have been on? No, because every struggle, every painful situation and every mistake I encounter is a key to success and happiness for my future. We just have to choose to see it for what it is; Life experience, not a life sentence.

I started writing this book when I was seventeen. I still had a big hill to climb. The hill was so big I couldn't comprehend how high it was at that point.

I am grateful that I didn't publish my story until now, almost ten years later, because I can now share the learnings from the uphill road I walked, sometimes almost crawled. These are the learnings that freed my mind and soul. I am only proud and grateful for everything life has taught me. I am proud to share what actually helped me to go from being a girl without any confidence, self-love or self-respect into being a free girl who sees the beauty in myself, others and in the world.

Sometimes, it can be so fucking frustrating when you are in the middle of a learning process; when you only see a pile of shit and feel like the whole world is against you. It can be hard to realise when you are in the middle of that smelly pile, that what you experience is something you will be grateful for in the future because it will teach you valuable life lessons. Everything that happens to us and all the emotions we feel, even the unwanted ones, are actually tools that we will be able to use in the future for greatness and happiness. So breathe and invite your patience along for when things feel a bit hard.

Your future is a question mark and that's a great thing.

So many times I wanted to get a glimpse of my future, to see if it was worth pushing through all the shit. If I had of been able to see myself now, and all the good things that were to come, I would've pushed through with my chin high.

I let myself out in words, through words. Writing is how I connect with my inner creativity, my source. I feel as if I can paint up any picture through my words. I can dream through letters and, with my words, make my dreams come true.

My writing has no rules. Instead, I followed the flow of my own tongue. I wish that as you read my book, you feel it as an expression of what is truly going on within me. I wish that when you read my story, you can connect to it and break free from the rules. This is the story about me, but also about us. This is a story about being imperfectly perfect for you, not for anyone else.

I write this book through love and a sincere wish to be free from time, made up musts, people pleasing and fakeness.

I hope you read as I write. With truth.

Maya.

Let's break some shit down before we start:

How to read this book

This book is written with my teenage panic and insecurity in mind – it is what I wished I understood, those times I thought that I did nothing right, or when I thought that I wasn't good enough for anyone. I channel that girl and through this book, I help her understand that freedom and love are everywhere.

My wish is that this book will help you to connect to places within yourself that you might have forgotten how to access or mightn't ever have had the access to before.

Grab a notepad and keep it on hand while reading. I have included some mind opening exercises, Hot Tips, at the end of each section. As you learn you can also start to think for yourself and see how you can be your own friend and connect to the best version of yourself.

What are the Hot Tips?

The Hot Tips have been created with the inspiration I find in the world all around me; the books, podcasts and interviews that have helped me reflect and find my way home to who I really am.

At the back of this book, I have included a list of those sources so you can read them or visit the online channels to watch and get more inspiration. There is one thing all these inspiring mentors teach;

You have to get lost to be able to find yourself and find your way home.

That is one reason why I believe mistakes are such an important part of living and learning; because it is through your mistakes, when you get lost, that you will learn about what you appreciate, like, don't like, love and don't love. It is through getting lost, you grow.

By getting lost and losing who you are I don't mean getting physically lost or just going shit crazy to prove a point – really getting lost happens naturally, without us even realising it. It is not a thing we can force or organise, it's not even hard to do, although it might take some work to find your way home. Sometimes you might need a little push in the back to get un-lost again. The most important thing is that you **want** to find your way back. Wanting and believing are essentially the only tools you need and you are set for a life of getting lost and discovering where you are again.

I ask myself the Hot Tip questions, whenever I feel lost on my way. They have given me confidence and an excited feeling to be the most **me** I can be in every situation (trust me when I say I have spent most of my life trying to be as little me as possible.) Being more me is so much better!

I have realised, and keep realising, that I have been lost on so many levels. I've even been lost in multiple ways at the same time. Through opening up my mind and soul to new ways of living, thinking and being, through asking myself the right questions, reflecting on my life and my reality, I keep finding my way back home. That's what this book is for.

It is a way of finding your way back home to who you truly are.

I really recommend that you start asking yourself the Hot Tip questions and tune into that inner home that will guide you towards your own true self and the confidence that comes with it.

After reading my story I hope that you find a new friend in yourself, so that everywhere you go you are walking hand in hand with the confidence, love and truth inside of you. It is my wish that you and you will live together forever.

So, grab a pen and a notepad; it's time to get to know yourself!

SECTION 1

WHO YOU ARE AND WHY YOU DO SHIT

This section is about trying to fit in and forgetting who you truly are in the process of doing so.

MAYA KIUSALAAS

IT ALWAYS STARTS WITH A HOODIE

I got 1000 Swedish kronor (about $100) for my 13th birthday with a pile of wrapped gifts. Quantity was everything then. I counted my presents like a spoilt child. I have no idea how I became that sort of child, my parents never taught me that material things were important. I cried because I didn't get enough presents for birthdays and Christmases. My brothers were the opposite, they got upset when my parents went outside of their budget to show them love with gifts. They didn't need material things to be happy, but I compared my gifts with everyone else's and always wanted what I didn't get.

So this birthday I woke up to the usual pile of gifts on the kitchen table. I had woken up early with my whole stomach filled with this buzz of excitement. It was MY birthday, and I needed this WE-shirt (a Swedish skateboard brand that was very popular). All the people I believed to be "cool" had them in school. In Sweden, we don't have school uniforms, so every day was sort of a runway showdown. I thought that people cared about what I did and wore, but the truth is that everyone was too busy thinking what everyone else cared about, so actually, we were all just thinking about ourselves. *"Please, please, please, can I just have a WE shirt?"* I had asked my parents a million times and they always said no. I was crying, I was angry. I needed to be a part of the group of people that had those shirts. I needed it to feel like I was good enough – that I was like them.

My parents didn't understand how you could put that much weight into a seriously overpriced hoodie. Especially since it was probably made in those factories that treated their employees like absolute shit. Shit on a level I couldn't even begin to relate to. I only saw status and a place to belong. I only saw a key to fitting in. I wanted people to look at me and think that I had what they had and give me that nod that told me that they could see that I "got it". I just wanted to look and feel like I had the money to buy that fucking shirt. To be honest, my parents didn't really have that much money to put on a single garment that they knew I would grow out of within a year. I didn't care. I thought the hoodie could give me the confidence to be me in school. That was what I was buying - confidence. I was constantly looking for outside sources and material things to give me confidence. I never knew that I could look to find that inside.

I walked into the store with my envelope of money, with my friend who had two shirts already, and I felt so relaxed. I felt like it was okay for me to be in the store now because I had the money and intention to buy a shirt this time. I also felt anxious because, deep inside, I probably knew that it was a fake thing, that I probably shouldn't spend that much on one shitty hoodie, a fake confidence, but I had to buy it anyway. I was starving to fit in and the hoodie would give me some nourishment. It was a surviving mechanism.

When I wore that shirt I felt protected, for a while. It lasted for as long as the shirt felt new, then I was on to the next thing that could make me feel included. If I only could've realised that I was included before the shirt, without the shirt. I inserted that feeling of being protected into the shirt, not to myself. If I would've been able to shift it around to see that the shirt had nothing to do with the real me I would've been able to feel protected and confident all the time.

I had fallen into living by the unwritten rules.

You know the unwritten rules, right? Unwritten rules are a type of trend that people adopt to be the same as everyone else. Some rules you follow knowingly, sometimes it's automatic. Each culture has its own unwritten rules and trends that are 'important' that we have to follow or else we will be left out.

The thought of not fitting in scares most of us so much we will do almost anything to adapt, so that we will not be left out.

When we take on the unwritten rules we can lose who we truly are – we lose the connection to our **authentic self** (the person you would be no matter where you are in this world, no matter who you are surrounding yourself with – the feeling inside of you which is aware of all the other feelings) - and we are reduced to a product of the society we live in. We become lost and cheap. The unwritten rules are everything that will make us feel as if we are a part of a group. It is trends in clothing and accessories, such as bags and bangs and slang. It's the photos we upload and share with the world that look just like everyone else's photos, it's the stories we tell and the ones we hide. There are rules out there that we are not even aware of that we are following.

We do it because we think it makes us happy. But does the happiness of being a part of a group come from deep within, or is that feeling just the lack of fear of not being left out? That depends on you and the group.

I want to know the real you. The world wants to know the real you. What did you really want to take a photo of? What did you really want to say? What would you really like to wear? Ask yourself, what would the situation be like if you followed your own path?

Hot Tip

I wish I understood that those rules I lived by were the ones that made me feel like I didn't belong. The ones that made me feel as if me as a person wasn't worth anything unless I had the right "stuff". I wish I knew about the unwritten rules and how unimportant they really were to my confidence; because when I started to follow them I started to feel fake, only instead of stopping, I came back for more. I needed more things to fit in – and the more things I believed that I needed, the more fake I felt. Still, I didn't get it. I didn't get that the whole reason I was feeling fake was because I put my confidence outside of myself – in things, not in actions.

*I invite you to **question the unwritten rules of life**, whatever they might be for you. The unwritten rules exist everywhere in the social world, in groups and clubs, in movies, in magazines. It's the places where we are taught and influenced by others on how to act, how to talk, how to be and live in a certain way in order to 'fit in'.*

Question the unwritten rules.

The thing about these rules, (this fake idea of fitting in), is that they only work if YOU believe in them!

You might think it's impossible to go your own way and do your own thing. It's not. It's so easy not to follow the trend and only do what actually comes naturally to you. ==You just have to find a way of being aware of when you are doing things just to fit in and when you are doing things because it makes you feel good all the way into your soul.==

==*Find your own culture and core.*==

In this book, I invite you to put what you think and feel and do up to the test and see for yourself what's real. **You might actually feel less left out as soon as you stop trying to fit in** *and just do whatever feels good for you. When you start to question WHY you do the things you do and start doing things because YOU want to do them, you will start to separate yourself from the mass that just absorbs all trends on autopilot. You will start living with a purpose of being the best, happiest, proudest and most excited version of yourself. (OMG!)*

Follow your own path with confidence.

In this book you will be able to open up to another truth about body image and social rules and realise that you don't have to follow any rules, only the ones from inside, if you want to feel at home within.

Be a trendsetter.

What if doing your own thing inspired others to do their own thing? What if your new individual thing is so naturally cool everyone wants to do it? What if it allowed you to develop deep and lasting friendships, or maybe even relationships?

What if you find your dream job and never 'work' another day in your life?

What if you felt in control of your life and happy with yourself? *Isn't all that worth asking the question of what am I doing this for?*

P.S. the answer should always be: "because I love it!"

Action:

1. Set a timer for three minutes. Write down all the unwritten rules about how you think society needs you to behave, what you need to have to fit in today.

   e.g. This can be a clothing brand, a phone, a style of dressing, a haircut, hair colour, TV series, what you do on weekends to fit in – Anything you can think of that you believe that everybody knows.

START YOUR TIMER and write!

2. Imagine now that you don't know any of the rules. For a couple of minutes let's pretend that you know nothing about how to behave in and outside of school and/or work. You don't know what is cool to wear or do – all you are left with is your connection to your emotions and how things make you feel!

Set the timer for another three minutes, close your eyes and just think about if there were no unwritten rules. What would that be like? Would how you act around other people change?

3. In a couple of sentences, write down how you think that your friends would describe the way:

    a)   you make them feel around you?

b) you would like to make them feel around you?

Are the answers the same? If not, what can you change about how you think and act to get the outcome you really want?

Remember, what you think about is what you get in life so if you want positive stuff, you need to think positive stuff in your head. If you want fun times you need to make room for fun times in your mind and daily schedule!

MAYA KIUSALAAS

LIFE IS PISS

My diary. Age 13

"Who the fuck wants to listen to me? I'm just a disgusting, ugly teenage girl who does nothing right. Why would anyone listen to someone like me? Guys don't like me. Probably none of my friends either. I'm probably just the shadow who nobody really wants to be with. I do everything for attention. I make my own bruises, cuts. I don't know; I like it when people feel sorry for me. On Saturday I didn't eat any breakfast... then I felt dizzy, but I didn't want to eat because I wanted to faint so that people would feel sorry for me. Love is piss. Everything is piss."

That wasn't me. Not really. That was a girl who felt like she didn't fit in. That was a very lost, very little me.

When I feel sad and anxious, I also feel lost in space, time and within myself. When I felt lost like that, I used to look to my friends or to society for answers. If you sometimes feel like that, you might go searching for external things like I did, to find ways to fake it (without even knowing that you are faking it); in what you wear, how you act, what you do – anything that makes you feel like you are found. You might put all your energy into trying to 'get it right', only that can make you feel more lost or like a fraud than when you started. You might even start to think it's your fault that you don't fit in. You might start to really believe;

> **"There is something wrong with me!"**

What I learned, when I found that home inside of me, through really getting to know myself (without looking at what other people are doing and comparing my journey to theirs), was that there was never anything wrong with me. I just didn't know myself in that moment, that's all. It's hard to try to get to know yourself when you don't really ask questions, like you do when you get to know a new friend. That's what this book is for. This is a new way of interacting with yourself that will help you get to know your real self like a new friend.

Today, if I feel uncomfortable in a situation, I sort of love it because it allows me to get to know myself on an even deeper level. I can ask myself, "Why did I feel like that around those people?" and, "If I could go back there and relive the same situation and connect to the real me, how would that have changed how I felt and behaved in that time and space?" You can literally learn something about yourself in every situation.

Most of the time when I get lost, it's because I am comparing myself to the people around me and listening to that inner paranoia in my head and devaluing what I can bring to a situation or a group of people – I forget what, and who, I am and remember only what I am lacking.

As soon as I realise that this is what I am doing I instantly get back home to myself and what I know is really me.

When I think about it truthfully and ask the right questions I can reflect and see how I could have handled that situation with pride and confidence. Then I can maybe say what I truly wanted to say or maybe I see that I can be quiet and calm and not say anything at all. In every situation like that, I've learnt something about myself that I didn't know or that I had forgotten.

Hot Tip

If I could travel back in time, I would start figuring out who I truly was by putting focus on what I am, what I like and who I'd like to be, instead of putting all my energy into trying to be who I thought everybody else was. <u>I would give myself the confidence to actually care about what I know is true for me. I'd see what is true in my world and in my heart, and then I would live for and with people who want to see the same thing or accept me for what I believe.</u>

But how do you do that? That just sounds like a bunch of cliché words and quotes? Back then I didn't believe "follow your dreams" was actually something that you could do. I thought that people who loved their life and what they were doing <u>were just lucky</u>. What I realise now is there is nothing worthwhile in fitting in and following what other people are doing. There is nothing worthwhile in caring about what other people think about you if you are empty. If you are feeling empty I'm guessing it's because you do these things. That's the truth, and when you try doing things differently, when you feel different, you will know it.

Do what you really like to do.

As soon as you start following what is true to you, a whole new world of possibilities will open up. I know I make that sound too easy and maybe you are panicking right now thinking, 'I can't just be myself! That's impossible.' It's not as bad as you think. You're not as bad as you think. Start as soon as you can because life will keep being piss until you do.

And btw: <u>never be ashamed of the people who you love and the people who love you;</u> they are the real people you need to care about, not people you semi-know or strangers on the fucking street that you will never see again.

Action:

Think about how people make you feel.

1. Pick three people that you are spending a lot of time around and write down how you feel when you are with them.

2. Ask yourself WHO makes you feel like that; is it them or have you gotten used to feeling that way around them? If you don't like how you feel, how can you change it?

> **Note: you don't owe anybody anything**

You being you is everything you need to be. When you stop acting as if you <u>owe people</u>

something for being in their company you realise that you already bring something good.

3. Write down what you bring that's good. Find five things that you bring to others.

You are already worth being around. You are already likeable, lovable and worthwhile. Just knowing that means you can be more you. The more you do that the better you will feel, no matter who you are talking to.

Being a people pleaser robs you of yourself. It is when you try to please others by acting to what you think they'll like, that you feel weak, fake, lost and like a fraud. It's not about how they make you feel, it's about how you choose to feel when you are around them.

Be yourself. Be in the moment. When you are connected to what is going on inside you and you let go of all expectations, that's when you can be free in any company.

4. Write down five things you dream of doing or being. It can be anything as long as you are only doing it for YOU. Think about what you need to start doing right now to get to that dream one day. (The more you start dreaming of what the real you is dreaming of, the easier it will get to navigate inside of you).

BEING YOURSELF

Being yourself sounds so abstract, who are you? And who am I? Shouldn't this be a really easy question to answer? It's okay if you are lost right now. Most people are!

Today when I think of who I am I think of what makes me happy. I am the choices I make and what I choose to settle with. I am Maya and everything that links back to her. I am full of love and I want to believe that everyone can live with love too if they choose to. I am honest which means that I say when I love things around me but also when I don't. I have weaknesses I am trying to be aware of, but I don't let those weaknesses define me. Instead, I try to become stronger through becoming more aware of those weaknesses and talk about them openly and honestly. I am proud to admit my flaws. The hardest part of writing down who I am now is that tomorrow I might, and probably will, have a slightly different answer for you. Who I am today in this moment is going to be different every time. We are like energy, constantly flowing, and we need to find a way of living in that flow and allow for changes to happen.

Back when I always felt lost I would've answered that I was Maya, but I would've had a harder time telling you who Maya was. I would've told you what she wasn't and defined her on what she didn't like. The old Maya was constantly trying to find new ways of changing who she was. She read all the weight loss articles and "how to act to get what you want" tips. She thought that, if she only looked "better" and acted like she was entitled to more, she would feel okay with who she was. She believed that loving who she was based on the question of, do other people love her. She thought that if she could look and act the part then it would be 'all good'. Never did she stop and ask herself "If these people didn't exist and if I didn't have to completely change the atmosphere around me – who would be left and what would that person like to do with her life".

When push comes to shove we find that most people in the Western world feel lost about who they are. They are confused about where they are going, even where they have just come from, not just once, but many times in their life. Even if we don't feel lost we can still believe that it's not okay to be ourselves, it's not okay to express ourselves because society will reject us. Wait, what? **Is that really the truth or is it**

just something we choose to believe so that we don't have to take matters into our own hands and take ownership over our own lives?

Yes, you can be yourself. Yes, you can express yourself.

What we need to do is to relearn how to dream big again (like we did when we were kids) and believe that we deserve to enjoy life. We need to relearn that it is more than okay to enjoy ourselves – that life is our own creation.

At some point early on we get taught not to listen to our own truths. We are raised as a collective, in a society. We are a mass. For that to work we must make sacrifices when it comes to individuality.

You can get your individuality back RIGHT NOW. All you have to do is take a look at what you think and what you feel and what you do and come to an agreement with yourself and see what you are willing to sacrifice and not. It is when we completely surrender to all the trends, should, musts and rules that we bury our individuality and become empty. We become 'them'.

To get back to you, you need to go out and make shit happen in the way that you want and need and dream of.

And yes, it's a bit harder at first, but being able to breathe, feed and live for yourself will give you the opportunity to be free in life, free with who you truly are supposed to be. Free within a system of unwritten rules.

Being yourself means, to me, that you are spending time doing what fulfils you and what makes you the best version of yourself. It means saying what you want to say without thinking or worrying about what other people might think. Being yourself means acting in a way that makes you feel at home inside. When you are who you feel comfortable being, your soul will award you with grace, gratitude, confidence, calm and awareness because you have learnt how to truly love and respect yourself.

I'm telling you this because I have reached this place. It's not just cliché words typed up. I was that girl doing all the 'right things,' the trendy things, and being so miserable and confused that I lost my excitement for living. I was so scared of getting disappointed that I stopped dreaming, I thought that if I didn't dream I wouldn't get disappointed. What happened was that my whole life more or less became a disappointment.

Now I have found that place where I am me all the time, stuff everyone else, I do my thing and it works! It's the best feeling in the world and I want for you to be here with me. All you need is a little bit of self-love.

Hot Tip
Finding self-love.

To me, self-love is when you are not thinking less of yourself. When you see beautiful and good things within other people you don't use that as a tool to see what they have and you haven't. You allow others to be amazing in their way without letting that be a reflection of any lack in yourself, because you have incomparable amazingness too. Self-love means, to me, that you care enough for your body and soul that you actively listen to its needs, like you'd listen to your best friend's needs.

Self-love is to be able to take a compliment and own it without questioning if it is true. It is to feel as if you are good enough and not constantly thinking stuff like "if I only become more like... or could look more like... then I will love myself".

Self-love is when you respect yourself enough to realise that you deserve to feel good, be happy and healthy, instead of thinking about all the reasons why you shouldn't feel good. You believe all the reasons why you should feel amazing – you are alive! Self-love is to allow yourself to be and do what makes YOU happy!

Action:

1. Write down what you think it means to "be yourself"?

2. On a separate page; write down three things:
    a) you are proud to have achieved
    b) you are good at
    c) you love (anything you love in life)

3. Write down five people who make you feel proud to be yourself.

4. Call one of them and ask them what they think it means to "be yourself".

EMBARRASSMENT

There was a time where I was so embarrassed of where I was from and what I didn't have that I would walk meters in front of my parents on the street, pretending that I didn't know who they were.

I remember my mum as the most confident person on earth. She always wore ugly clothes and self-made beanies and she wore them with pride. Like that black and white beanie with earflaps that she hand-made. She loved that beanie and wore it until the fabric was no longer a fabric, I am pretty sure it was just stardust in the end. When she came and picked me up from school, waving her arms in the air with her black armpit hair showing I was so happy to see her… until I understood that women should not have black armpit hair in this society. I cried and cried until she decided to start shaving her armpits and her legs. She had black hair on her legs and used to spray chamomile on them to bleach them. She then had golden leg hair with a touch of orange. I begged to all the gods in the world that nobody would see me out with my family.

The worst days, days that would have me stressed for weeks, was when my parents had to come to school for meetings or some activity. I got stomach cramps. My anxiety was through the roof. I thought that our family was so lowly that other people would look at us and laugh. I thought that if strangers saw my parents, they would know that I was some fraud. I felt that they would be able to see right through me.

Then I decided that being so obvious about it was more embarrassing. If people could see me pretending and being ashamed and in pain about my family it was so much worse and so totally fake. So when I got a couple of years older, I started to get loud and laugh a lot when I was out in public with my parents. I put on an act, pretending that we were the funniest people on earth. I hugged and kissed them, and then when we were at home, behind closed doors, I put down my act and became the angry teenager again.

Hot Tip

I wish I could see that status is just a thing created by insecure people, and trying to fit in with them by buying the same clothes as them is just buying friendship or status or happiness. **I don't want people to like me for what I am wearing; I want people to like me for me when I am true to who I am.**

If I could go back in time and give myself some tips, it would be to stop wasting time looking at what I didn't have and start exploring what I actually did have and be grateful for it.

I didn't have to pretend, I already had the most fun family that I could laugh and joke with, who gave me so much love. I did have a lot of genuinely good friends too, that I know cared for me like I cared for them, with or without that fucking "WE" hoodie. For some reason, I tended to put my focus towards the friends that probably didn't care about me as much, because they were "cooler", but definitely not nicer, and that is something that I wish I could change.

Now I always choose to be around people who let me express myself. They would never tell me how to act, dress or be in the same way that I never would ask them to change who they are for me. If someone tries to change who I am, I simply let them know that who I am is not up for negotiation - because I love being me.

Action:

1. Have you ever thought that you needed to have something (like a phone, a garment, wear a certain brand) to fit in and be accepted by your friends? Make a list of the things you think are important outside and another list of

things you think are important inside. Be honest. If you could have people like you for just one list, which one would you choose?

2. When you buy something or want something, do you want it because you honestly love it or because you think about what other people will think of you when you wear it/use it/have it?

Every time you buy something, ask yourself if you are buying it for yourself or to "look good" in front of other people.

What if it was an internal value or quality they wanted, would you work as hard to do that thing as you would to buy something?

If you were marooned on an island what would you contribute to get off it or to survive (I bet you it's not a WE hoodie!)

3. Write down the qualities you look for in a friend? Do you look for that in yourself too? Is this already who you are?

4. Do you care about what other people think of you? Write down why this is important to you?

5. Write down as many friends as you can think of that would be with you no matter what you have or don't have.

    Send them each a text now saying how much you appreciate them for letting you be who you are!

MAYA KIUSALAAS

THE FUCKING FORD

It's hard to try to fit in with the group of people in WE hoodies when you have a mother like my mum. I love her for making it hard for me. I love her now, but back then I was flat out paralysed with shame. Forget her hairy armpits and the chamomile-bleached leg hair, allow me to introduce you to our summer-vehicle; the Ford.

We rented a car to drive down to Italy with my uncle, his wife and my cousins. A huge square Ford that could fit nine passengers. It was bright red, and before the trip my mum decorated it inside with jungle animals and plastic flowers. She used off cut material to sew individual pockets that she tied to each seat (they were actually very handy on such a long trip). After the holiday we were supposed to return the van and move on with our lives, but Mum and Dad loved it and ended up buying that hippie-van.

I honestly don't remember how many years we were stuck with the Jungle Car but everybody in our neighbourhood soon knew that that was the Kiusalaas-family car. Oh, the agony! Okay, so I can admit that it was fun when Dad could drive all our friends around together. But it wasn't about what my friends thought, what mattered was what strangers thought. You know, the people you know but you don't know well, what did they think about the car we drove? They must think I'm such a loser. I couldn't stand the thought of other people seeing the van and thinking that we were different and weird. I wanted to be normal.

I wanted to just have a fucking Volvo.

Dad parked the car in different places around our apartment block (we didn't have a secure spot). Over time one of the side windows was smashed, graffiti was painted on the whole sliding door. The Jungle Car looked a bit sad with plastic over the broken window and someone's tag stamped on the side.

When we drove up to our friend's farm and opened the side door, it actually fell off, and we had to spend the first hour of our visit trying to put the door back on the car. 'Grand entre'.

One day I walked around with my friends on a break in between classes. There were a lot of people around. We were walking from the lolly store when I saw it, the Jungle Car was coming towards us. I froze inside. I did everything in my power for my friends not to see it, only there was no way to avoid it. I stormed off, and Mum drove past touting the horn with all her love and happiness. She was so excited to see my friends and me. I just wanted that fucking jungle hippie car out of my life.

Illustration: Arvo & Inka Kiusalaas

Hot Tip

I dare you to think about all the good things around you. Think about and appreciate everything you do with your family; whatever your family constellation may look like, and remember what makes you all laugh together. Think about how you view other people's families. Maybe you sometimes compare your family to others, dreaming about having what they have. Think about what you have in the same way, and instead of looking for what is missing, look for what amazing things that are there instead.

I realise now that I was scared of people reacting to me and my family's approach with pettiness. I wanted more for my family. I believed that if anyone saw what we didn't have, they would look down on us. Only when I shifted focus and saw what a loving, creative and open family we were, I started to be proud of being a part of us. I loved the fact that our door has always been open for everyone. We always had enough food to feed an army of friends that basically felt as at home in our house as we did. My parents always welcomed our friends, even the ones they didn't quite understand. Once I started to pay attention to what amazing people they really are and felt grateful for what we had as a family I stopped caring about what strangers might think and how people might judge us for what we didn't have, because I knew what we did have, and what we had was love.

As I got older, I learnt that I was brought up in a very cool and unique family. We always had dinner together, talking about literally everything you can talk about. Every weekend Dad woke us up with breakfast on the table, and we could sit for hours refilling our enormous coffee cups and just talk about life. My parents have done everything they could to make us genuinely happy, and they have never complained once about things that they haven't been able to do. I now wish that I wouldn't have complained so much to them about what I didn't have because I know that they always did their best to give us everything that we needed. They always put us first, and me not seeing that, constantly wanting more and more, and more made me super ungrateful, and that ungratefulness made me super unhappy.

Action:

1. Write down ten things about the person/people who care for you that you are grateful for. Do they cook for you? Do they drive and pick you up from places? Are they working so that they can give you a roof over your head? Do they care about you when you are upset? Do they want you to have the best life possible? (share this with them in a text, call, note or in person, if you dare!)

2. Write down six things that you bring to a group that will make you feel strong in yourself. (You can even ask people what they think if you find this hard in the beginning!)

Remember to forget about what you think that other people might think you should answer and really try to feel what your emotions are telling you. Why do I say that? Because what you think they think is not necessarily true. People act in the craziest ways that just don't make sense. You can't read minds to know why they do stuff!

e.g.
1. I always bring honesty, and that makes me feel free, and others too, because then they can be honest as well.
2. I share things that make people laugh.
3. I care about everyone in a group and want everyone feeling welcome.

Now that you have come to the end of this section, you have some fun and challenging things to consider. Are you letting what you believe other people think, stop you from treating the people you love and who love you with acceptance and appreciation, like I did?

Now, let's really focus on the good fucking shit!

Connect to your true and happy self by remembering exciting things that make you feel free in a group of people or by yourself.

It's your turn!

SECTION 2

DREAMING OF REACTIONS

This section is about questioning what you identify yourself with, finding your passions and figuring out what kind of attention you are after.

MAYA KIUSALAAS

THINGS THAT HURT

I've always survived by the reactions I received from people. In school when I made my wounds and squeezed out blood, I felt calm from the reaction people had. I felt calm when they noticed that I was bleeding. Maybe I felt calm when I could physically see that *I* was hurting? When I used my asthma spray and people got curious of my asthma, I felt visible. I felt like I had a reason to be noticed.

It was as if I tried to force people to feel for me because I didn't trust that they would without help. I thought they needed reasons to see me. I think that is most likely why my inner chaos felt somewhat relieved when I later developed anorexia. People could see that I was suffering. They could see me, even if it wasn't the person I truly wanted to be, at least I was noticed.

It wasn't as if I thought, "Oh, nobody is noticing me, let's make a wound". I didn't realise what I was doing to begin with; I just scratched, squeezed and felt sorry for myself. Then calm. I felt as if I was allowed to feel sorry for myself if others felt sorry for me. Throughout my whole life I have been screaming to the world "See me, hear me, feel me!" and I only realised years later that I actually wasn't screaming for the world to see me, I was screaming to myself.

It was only when I started to see and feel myself, I could start to make a difference.

I've always nursed myself in strange ways. I loved getting injured and get bandages to show off. Sometimes I went to kindergarten with a bandage wrapped around my skull or arm for no reason. Sure it was fake, but I still loved it. I remember the smell of our compression wrap, liniment and elastic, a sweet and healing scent. When I was six, I tried to break my own legs so that I could get crutches, which didn't work, but a girl in school had an electric wheelchair and a set of crutches she needed and she let me borrow them sometimes. I loved it, and I remember wishing that I actually needed them.

It was like my subconscious was seeking healing attention, or maybe just any kind of attention. I didn't know how to make people love me just the way I was, because I didn't love myself that way. By injuring myself, I guess I had a reason for getting attention.

Once I finally understood that I don't have to be injured, sad and in pain, for people to see me, it opened up a whole new path for me to explore. I learnt that I don't want people to experience my company as heavy, sad and depressing, because in my deepest most genuine person that is the opposite of who I truly am. I don't need people to feel sorry for me anymore, thank god! I want people to feel stronger by being with me, and I want people to be inspired to feel good around me. I love laughing and being silly, so it doesn't make sense to beg people to feel sorry for me with self-made wounds.

I realised that by being the best, happiest and strongest I can be in each moment, I can be the person who makes someone else feel good rather than the opposite.

Every person is different, I promised at the start we are all unique, and so are our reasons for doing the weird shit we do. I used self-harm to get attention, to be seen, but for somebody else, it might be because it is the only way they know how to cope with their emotional pain. Right then and there, we can only do what we know to do.

Ask yourself: "Why am I doing this?"
Ask yourself: "What is a different way to express my (name your emotion)?"

Unless you try different things what you know will stay the same.

Always remember that you are not alone, even though it might feel like it from time to time. There are always people out there whose passion is to try to help, find them through people you trust, through help lines or your doctor.

Hot Tip

You can only do what you know to do in a situation, it is not until you learn a new way you will be able to change. There are so many different ways of expressing your emotions. Think about it, your physical body is not your emotions, so maybe you can try to find a different outlet for your emotional pain. Here is a list of things you might want to try to do if you ever feel like you don't know how to cope with your emotions:

1. Get help. Call a doctor, psychiatrist, help line or any adult you trust.

2. Cry. Allow yourself to cry and feel sad. Find peace and calm in your emotions. Love crying

and see it as for what it really is - you are letting your emotions out.

Sometimes I get so frustrated with myself because I want to feel different to what I am feeling in the moment. I don't accept what I feel so instead of dealing with the original feeling I just add frustration to it. It gets layered up and pushed down and finally it gets really shitty. Instead; try to let whatever it is up and be done with it.

3. Paint how you feel

4. Write poems

5. Write down what you feel, why you are feeling what you are feeling (if you know why) and what you think will make you feel better.

6. Listen to music.

7. Go out for a run or walk

8. Try letting your emotions out through boxing or Muay Thai.

9. Write a letter to your pain and explain how it is making you feel.

MAYA KIUSALAAS

WHAT IF PEOPLE ACTUALLY SEE (THE REAL) ME?

Remember those kids in school who honestly burn for something, the ones who had a genuine passion? They knew who they wanted to be. They didn't compare their dreams to others because their dreams were real. I wasn't one of those kids. My dreams were compared and judged all the time, by myself. They constantly changed and died. Like when I decided to become a police officer just because I would be allowed to exercise at work, or when I wanted to create a happiness measuring app to have people see for themselves how important sleep, diet and exercise is to your overall happiness, or when I thought I could be the prime minister of Sweden even though I have never had an interest in politics – I just wanted to be someone I could say that I was.

I didn't value my dreams because they weren't real to me. I just tried to be like the people around me, and I thought that if I could be like them, then I would be "right". But I constantly felt "wrong". **The harder I tried to act like the people I surrounded myself with, the more uncomfortable I felt**, and I thought that I had to change and become even more like them in order to feel comfortable. **I now know that only by trying to be the most me-ish I can possibly be I would feel comfortable.**

What I know now is that the people who live for status and luxury, like I did, who look to outside things for confidence, were just too scared to be truly seen for themselves. They surrounded themselves with things that could protect them from being seen as vulnerable and real. They use status in the same way I used bleeding wounds, to be noticed, because what if being you isn't good enough, right? I tried to be like everyone else and never learnt how to actually connect to my own emotions trust my own intuition. I kept looking outside of myself for something that clearly comes from inside; the confidence to be me.

I lived in a competition. Like a game show. To gain that status we believed we needed to survive, my friends and I stood strong together and distanced ourselves from the people we thought were different. I see now that the whole friendship was built on constantly confirming what we weren't and who we didn't want to be. You know, when your common ground is to talk about what other people are doing wrong and find solidarity through that – that is when friendship isn't built on something solid; like love. We never talked about or aimed for who we wanted to be. The friendship and the status was built on a nothingness that lead us to be nothing. I thought that I could feel safe as long as I also became all the things that I wasn't. But then I was no one. No wonder I felt lost. No wonder I was in emotional chaos.

I know that my need for this hurting kind of attention is directly linked to lacking the confidence to truly express myself. It is scary to put all that you are passionate about out there. To actually say "fuck it" to what the people around you are doing and do what'd actually do if no one else was around. Being hurt was a way for me to be seen without risking people not liking what they see in me. It brought out other people's empathy, and that made me feel good. But when I finally connected to my own inner strength and started to be the person I truly was, I realised that there is nothing better than the feeling of putting one hundred per cent you out there in the world and not caring about what reactions you do get from people.

When I finally started doing things for myself and not for others, I realised it is worth a million times more than the combined empathy I have

gotten throughout my whole life from making myself suffer.

I am aware of the fact that I do like attention from people's reactions. That doesn't have to be a bad thing as long as I also listen to what tools I use in order to get that attention. If I ever hear myself trying to get attention through injuries or saying something negative about myself, I know to take a step back. I have to ask myself, "What am I scared of really revealing?" and I shift from trying to make people feel sorry for me to the confident, free person I know I can be.

I love to express my freedom to be who I want to be. I love shining light on the fact that false rules exist by stepping outside of them and being myself. Once I realised that I could choose to get attention through weakness and pity or through strength and freedom I experienced a new level of confidence. Now I am like a child, constantly testing boundaries. That is a part of me that I love and value. Through being me and questioning things that, "just are," I hope that others will do the same.

Hot Tip

You know when a person enters a room and the whole vibe shifts? They come with a good, happy and loving energy and people want to be around them because they make everyone feel a little better just by simply being safe, honest and proud to be themselves.

Then you know when someone comes into a room with a heavy energy, who doesn't know how to communicate their emotions and instead they try to connect to people through strong and heavy emotions; like sadness or pain. Have you sharing is

Everyone is sad, angry, frustrated and lost sometimes, and we should always be able to share how we truly feel in the moment. But sometimes we might use emotions just to get attention. We might not actually feel what we are projecting, it's just insecurity. When know you have a choice, it is up to you to choose to be that person that makes everybody feel good around you, or the one who brings down the energy in the room.

- *When you walk into a room, how do you want people to feel around you?*
- *How do you get other peoples attention?*
- *What do you want to talk about – the things you love, or the things you hate?*

- *Have you ever said something negative about yourself or somebody else just to get someone's attention? If yes, could you have got the same or even "better" attention through sharing something positive about yourself or someone else?*

By breaking down these questions of how you would like people to feel around you and figuring out happy and healthy ways of connecting to people you'll find that you influence the people around you to feel good as well.

If you feel sad, lonely, angry or upset; try to understand the feelings you are feeling and accept that you are feeling them for a while (know that they will not last forever). Try to get to know all of your feelings. Then, when you are done feeling something, figure out what feelings you would love to feel: Walk towards them through focusing on where you are going, not where you are at right now.

- *What do you want to feel? Pretend to live in that feeling for a while; what does your life look like when you feel that way, what do you do, who are you with, what do you talk about?*

- *What do you usually do to make you feel like you want to feel? (talk to a friend, go for a run, paint, write, go for a walk, listen to a song you love? – Do that)*

Action:

1. Write down ten things that usually get you in a good mood.

2. Keep it somewhere where you will remember it the next time you need it!

SO I AM NOT A FUCKING GYMNAST?

My emotional life went to shit when my passion for gymnastic died. I was a good gymnast, with a lot of potential to improve. I was in love with the group, the community around it and the discipline it demanded. I loved to always have something fun to look forward to every day, something I was working on and striving towards. I loved being upside down as much as possible. But when the training turned into more than a fun discipline and became a serious must, I couldn't see the point of it. It stressed me out rather than filling me with excitement. I was there for the love and community, but when winning competitions became the main reasons we trained, I lost my connection to the sport. But that wasn't all; I also lost my identity. Up until then, I had identified myself with and through my love for gymnastics, but when it became a burden, I had to break free.

For a long time, I felt so angry with gymnastics. I felt like the dynamic of the group changed and grew without me. I wanted them all to feel like I felt. I couldn't understand that just because I felt that gymnastics was there for fun, other people might want to actually progress and compete. I felt as if the trainers failed me because they didn't let me play around. I became a victim - they had taken my passion away from me through putting up rules I didn't want to follow. I wasn't ready or willing to sacrifice that bit of individual connection to the sport to be a part of that community and collective anymore.

Now I know that I could've said what I wanted and found a better fit for me, or take ownership that maybe gymnastics wasn't for me anymore. Maybe I had to look within and ask my heart (not my brain) what I would rather spend my time doing. What would make me feel excited and free? Maybe I was the one who had grown in a different direction, but it was too hard for me to see, so I blamed gymnastics instead.

When I lost gymnastics, I lost the guidance gymnastics gave me. I was in an ocean with no guidance at all, but I didn't quite understand that yet. I needed everything I had before, the rules for a reality built on love, not on competition. I needed the routines that made me feel happy and alive. I needed to know that I am doing things to feel the best I can feel and be the best person that I can be. I needed guidance in a chaotic world. I later learnt that I was on a constant search to find the path of least resistance.

When I lost that source, I lost my identity. I was swimming around trying to connect with people and with myself, but I had no idea how to do that. I tried to adapt to what I was taught to be the real world. But what I tried to adapt to was nothing real. I looked for groups of people who I believed could make me feel noticed and cool. I looked for people who could give me the confidence and identity that was suddenly missing.

I started comparing myself with others, looking for what they did 'right' and mimicking that. There were no instructions about how to connect to my own emotions and my own truth to figure out what was right for me. I didn't know how to ask for it. I don't even know if I realised that I was feeling lost. I only knew that I believed that other people were better and more worthy than I was. I believed that to be the truth.

Hot Tip

Don't create an Identity based on what you aren't. Figure out what you are, what makes you laugh and what you love about other people. What do you love doing? What places or situations make you feel free? How can you create a life where you wake up every morning to the feeling of feeling free to be you?

Action:

1. Write down five things that make you laugh.

2. Write down five things that you can talk about forever. (Explore those things more!)

3. Write down three situations, places, activities where you don't think about what other people think of you, where you just are the way you are and do the things you do because you love doing them.

4. What kind of person are you? What kind of person do you want to be?

If they are not the same, what steps can you take to change this?

Remember to also feel the answer in your body, through your emotions, rather than letting your brain tell you what you should answer.

SECTION 3

ANOREXIA AND SHIT

This chapter is about eating disorders and how they can occur from lack of self-love and confidence. It is about losing who you are in the search for love.

BIOLOGY CLASS IN YEAR EIGHT

I wore my pink H&M shirt and my Diesel Jeans with the fake Hugo Boss belt I stole from my brother. I covered my stomach with one hand as if that would make people see less of what I hated so much. It was spring, and we had the classroom window open. A cool breeze swept in through the room. I loved that feeling after such a long and dark winter, a winter that from time to time seemed endless. When you finally could see some signs of life in the trees. I loved that.

This year I couldn't enjoy the breeze or the spring light brought to us by the sun though. I couldn't enjoy the singing birds. What used to be the sign of hope didn't touch me in the slightest. I didn't feel any hope inside my body, I needed to escape it. I needed to be anyone but myself. I was done with me. At that time I was obsessed with food. I ate every three hours but tried to eat as little calories as possible. If I didn't eat something every three hours, I truly believed that my metabolism would shut down and I would get fat, immediately.

I looked up diets and tried to find shortcuts to become who I wanted to be through changing the way that I looked. I understand now that who I wanted to be wasn't anywhere to be found underneath the 5kg of my skin (that would be unhealthy for me to lose). But you can't just say that to a young girl who hates everything about herself and hope that she will get it; you have to help her understand it - from the inside and out.

My biology teacher, Keith, talked about eating disorders, anorexia, bulimia and about the warning signs. My best friend glanced over at me, but I was too busy taking notes to care about her worrying looks. This was my goal. To become as skinny and as sick as possible, so that I could love myself and so that people could see and understand the pain I was in. People would see me. It is so absurd to think that I actually sat there deciding to do this to myself. The year before this spring day I had become more and more obsessed and unsatisfied with the way I looked; through constantly looking for the wrong things with myself in the mirror. Day in and day out. This day wasn't the beginning, it was just the day all my negative self-talk truly manifested itself.

My head was a total mess. I felt anxious both when I ate something and when I didn't eat anything. It didn't matter what I did because whatever I ended up doing I convinced myself it was wrong. I couldn't win. It drove me completely crazy. After a trip to Zanzibar with my family, Mum really noticed that I was struggling. I was obsessive, angry and super stressed around food. Mum booked me into the anorexia and bulimia clinic the same night we got home from Zanzibar and I completely fucking panicked.

I wasn't sick! And I definitely wasn't skinny enough to be booked into an eating disorder clinic. What would people think in the waiting room, when I came in and I'm not really REALLY skinny? I'd take up time from someone who is really sick. They would see what a fraud I was. I felt nauseous. The meeting wasn't until February 14. That was one month away. I had one month to get skinny enough to see the eating disorder psychiatrist. The irony of that took me years to see.

What would the "real" girls think of me? I felt helpless, and at the same time, I felt so fake. I felt like I wasn't ill for real. I had chosen to be this way, but I couldn't, I wouldn't, I refused to gain weight. That would be worse than death. I had a controlling inner voice in my head that told me there was no turning back. I didn't deserve help.

I admired the really sick girls, the ones who actually deserved to be there. They weren't faking like I was. I looked at them and saw how fragile they were and wished I could tell them how strong I thought they were in their weakest moments. I didn't realise that I was admiring someone living in hell. Because that is what it is, just hell.

Hot Tip

Anorexia and all eating disorders are a sign of an inability to love and respect who you are. Back then I thought that I would accept myself only if I could change the way I looked, but the more I forced myself to change the unhappier I got.

This does not just apply to eating disorders – it's about the belief that you are not good enough the way you are, so you might think you have to change in order for you to accept yourself and for others to accept you too. Like getting plastic surgery, like the compulsive need to buy new clothes you don't need, like being in a relationship with someone who abuses you. It is all the same lack of feeling calm and pleased with who you are, in your own body.

I spent over ten years trying to change everything that was me. The only thing that finally made me really happy and content with myself was one day when I decided that I will not change who I am; because I can't. I will always be me, no matter what my outside will go through. My body is not me, so if my body changes; I will still be here.

*I decided that I will change the way I take care of myself. I will make my **here** worth it.*

Action:

1. Take a deep breath. Feel and connect to your emotions inside. If you were to pick a place inside of your body that you believe that YOU are (the force that feels happiness, sadness, excitement, empathy, frustration, love etc.) Where is that? Is it in your core? Your solar plexus? If you could describe it in words or in colours, how would you describe it? Is it fluffy, sharp or constantly changing? Play around with this as much as you like. I always get different answers when I try to connect to that place.

2. When you are connected to that place or those places inside of you, do you think that they will change if your outside changes?

3. Whenever you feel lost in this world – connect to that source of YOU-ness inside of you and know that you are never alone.

IDEALS & OBSESSIONS

My biggest role models in the world were healthy girls who did whatever they wanted to do, said whatever they wanted to say without looking at what other people thought of them. The girls I looked up to in my teenage years weren't celebrities; they were always people I knew. Like the daughter of our family friends who always made me feel confident just by being near her. Or the older gymnastics girls who could do things with their bodies I once dreamed of being able to do myself. I looked up to girls who did stuff by themselves without fear of being seen alone or with their parents without being embarrassed. It was that attitude of actually **not thinking about what other people would think of them** that inspired me, because it was what I lacked myself. Every single girl in my surroundings I looked up to and got inspired by were healthy, loving, kind and cool people – so why did I fight to become weak and skinny? Why did I hang onto my sadness and my fear like life itself depended on it?

Happy, confident and strong people don't constantly think about what other people think of them. Instead of asking, "What would X think if I do this/wear this/say this?" confident and happy people think, **"Is this what I really want?"** They wake up in the morning thinking about what is working out for them and what possibilities the day will bring. They are curious about what the world has to offer. Happy and confident people don't think about what they are lacking in life because they are too busy making use of what they actually have and working with that. Happy and confident people see what there is to live for. Sad and unconfident people see only what's missing and what they don't want to have in their life.

On that note, I wish that I'd kept looking up at those people who were truly happy and free to be themselves. I should have put my focus towards figuring out how they could be so happy instead of getting inspired by those who literally were killing themselves and starving. I should've set a goal to become the happiest girl on the planet. Why couldn't I see that being sick with anorexia wouldn't make me happy?

Why did I look for the unhappiest people for inspiration to find my happiness?

The more weight I lost the more obsessed with food and body image I became. I was completely absorbed with thoughts of food. It was all I could think about. It's not like I was just sitting around chilling, not feeling like eating and it's all easy. I used to go out for walks just to go from supermarket to supermarket staring at food. I walked around the aisles, like people who love art walk around in their favourite gallery. I knew the supermarkets we lived near better than the people who worked there. I read cookbooks as literature and I woke up in the middle of the night with an urge so strong to bake I couldn't go back to sleep before I had made blueberry muffins that I would never eat. My mind was so occupied by thoughts about weight and food that I didn't spend any time focusing on how to get happy. All I wanted was to love myself, and I thought that changing my body would help me achieve that, but all it did was the opposite. I should've focused on how to love me, not change me. I know that now.

I had a friend at that time who always got attention. People constantly told her how beautiful she was, and to me, it felt like all the guys in the world dreamed about her. We were inseparable. I lived in her shadow, at least that was what my insecurity told me. From the outside, and to her we were probably just two people being friends, no one better than the other in any way – the comparison happened in my own mind; that's where I decided that she was better than I was, it wasn't the truth. I can see now that I was jealous and adored her at the same time, but to me, she always complained about her body and looks; there was always something wrong. I thought that if she got all the attention and still thought that she wasn't beautiful enough, maybe I had to start looking at myself the same way she did, so I could be better and look more like her. I never stopped and valued what I had, I kept comparing myself to her and every other girl that wasn't me. After a couple of years I only knew who I was based on what I didn't have.

I was so insecure, which might sound strange because I was very outgoing and bubbly. The truth is, if you don't believe that who you are is enough and if you believe that you have to change to get accepted – you are insecure because you cannot see yourself as complete. I felt with my whole being that I had to change or I wouldn't be worth anything. Not love, not a life. I thought that I needed other people to tell me that they loved me, so I could love myself. I didn't realise that I needed to love myself for other people to love me more.

Complaining and looking for what was wrong with me became who I was. It made me see only ugliness and shit. Shit that didn't actually exist. I focused on the wrong things in the mirror and I got more and more obsessed. I had developed a slow self-hate that, over time was explosive.

Hot Tip

Feeling as if you have to change who you are and lack self-love is a sign that there is a wound that needs to be healed somewhere deep inside of you. That wound is bleeding out your confidence, happiness and self-love, and you need to find where that wound is, what has caused it and help it to heal. Wounds like that will heal through the realisation of your self-worth. ***You need to feel and trust that you are good enough by just being you.*** *You need to feel deep in your body (not think with your brain) what it is that makes you feel scared and lost and then understand that, while it is okay to feel that way, what is going to help you is connecting to your inner freedom of* ***choosing who you want to be and who you love to be?***

Instead of changing who you are; help who you truly are to be free as you would help your best friend in feeling that he/she is good enough just the way he/she is. Help yourself with love.

Action:

1. Every morning when your alarm goes off say out loud to yourself and connect to the emotions of feeling that "I am good enough the way I am and even if anyone tries to be like me – they can't because only I am me!"

2. Pretend that you are your own friend and tell yourself exactly what you would tell a friend that you love if that friend said to you that he/she believed that they had to change in order to be accepted by others.

I AM NOT MYSELF

I was staring at myself in the mirror in my room; I didn't know who I was anymore. I punched myself in the stomach again and again and again. My hate for myself and my body was so physical. I was screaming. Crying. Panicking. I felt like I was in the wrong body. It took over my life. I was such a happy girl to start with, I loved gymnastics and living, now I saw only what was wrong, what I hated. It was as if I was caught in the wrong body.

I stopped eating because I had developed this self-hate and I was punishing myself. **I had created this hate by talking shit about myself.** I thought that the only way I could be loved was to make people see that I was hurting. The more weight I lost, the unhappier I got with myself and at the same time my obsession with food completely took over my life. I cooked dinners for my family, stirring pots like a maniac for three hours before they got home from work and school. I lit candles and I looked at them eating, while I was battling with eating as little as possible. I didn't get my period. I had no energy. I had lost myself. I was just filled with this obsession with body image, food and hate. I was angry. So angry.

During my years of starvation, I started to nurse myself like I was my own baby. It was as if I subconsciously starved myself so I didn't have to grow up. I longed for self-love like I had when I was a child. I needed to love myself so I went back to a time when love was all there was. I bought a baby bottle so that I could drink warm gruel in bed every morning. I sipped on it like a baby, and it made me feel safe for a while. I started to watch the cartoons and TV shows I loved as a kid. I remember feeling so small and helpless in a beautiful way, like I needed Mum and Dad then, I needed their love. I needed my own love too, and that was nowhere to be seen.

Love wasn't the only thing I needed. I needed rules and order in my life to quiet the chaos of self-destructiveness I had invited into my life, into my head. I needed some way of feeling that I did well, I needed to feel as if what I did, I did for a good reason.

But there was no reason. I did what I did to look and feel sick, at the same time, I wished that I was happy and healthy. It made no sense. If I could have opened up my body, turned it inside and out for people to see what was going on emotionally, I don't think anyone would've been able to grasp it. My emotions, feelings and thoughts were in no order. They contradicted each other. I had no guidance on what to listen to. I had no truth in my life. I had a million different thoughts and emotions and I was suspicious of every one of them. I believed that everything that happened around me was a trick someone was playing on me. The arrows that were my inner compass were pointing in all the directions at the same time, it was spinning and spinning and spinning. I was disconnected from myself. It was like ten people from different cultures, different ages and different centuries were trying to come up with one way of living in peace together. Everyone wanted the other people to do it their way. It was just complete mayhem, and nothing ever got done, just voices screaming at each other. I was in a paralysed state of chaos.

When chaos exists, extreme order is like a paradise, to start with that is, so my eating disorders were a big relief to me because it created a kind of inner peace for a while. It shut the million voices up for a few seconds. I could breathe again. I had control, a purpose and routine again. But this extreme order slowly turned my life into imprisonment, punishment and guilt. It took away one of my highest values; freedom.

Hot Tip

*When you are depressed, anxious and full of self-hate, your mind is constantly focusing on finding things that are wrong with you. To help change that negative spiral, **you need to change your focus**. Start telling yourself things that you like about yourself, write lists, write nice things on your mirror. Anything, **even things you might not believe at that time**. If you use all your time thinking about shit, you will feel like shit. Think about love, happiness and endless possibilities and you will see it because you spend your time thinking and focusing on it. Allow yourself to DREAM happy dreams and play with the absolute best-case scenarios!*

If it is hard to see anything good with yourself, you have to force yourself to think about good things about you. Sit down and focus your mind on things you like about yourself and the world and connect to those thoughts with emotions. Write good shit down. Anything from nice nails, happy laugh, good heart, fun-crazy brain. Think about all the good things that you have around you. Your family, friends, comfortable blankets, colourful flowers, fun TV, good books and music, etc. The more good things with and around yourself you can think of, the more you will find.

Never ever listen to people or voices in your head that talk shit about you. If you hear your own brain think, "I can't do that", "I am not as pretty as him/her" or "I wish I could look/be like that person", you have to stand your ground and protect yourself like you would protect a friend. Be your own friend, because those voices are full of shit.

Not liking myself didn't just happen overnight, I learnt from our culture, from friends, from everywhere. We have created a society together where we are immune to compliments. We fight them off like bugs because we are scared to take them in. We are scared that they are not real and that we will disappoint people. But they are real if we start treating them like they are. It is all about focus. When I started believing that everything good anyone had to say about me was a lie, then they became a lie, because I didn't believe them.

One of my biggest regrets in life is that I stopped telling myself, and believing how good and unique I am and how lucky I am to be alive. I stopped listening to what I loved, what was fun, who I had fun with. I started to listen to my ego, which came with shame and guilt, and I started to take life too seriously. I mean, life is super serious because it is real, but I started to change myself in order to fit in — I lost my ability to live in the flow of life.

Action:

1. Sometimes when we get anxious we tend to stiffen our whole body, almost seizing up without realizing it. Are you doing that? If you are, try to just shake our your whole body (look as silly as you need to), get your face involved and shake it out, maybe dance a little if you dare. Just make sure that your whole body is awake, relaxed and free.

2. Set the timer on your phone for five minutes, close your eyes and think about all the good things your body can do for you. Feel gratitude that you have legs to walk with, eyes to see with and arms to hug people you love with. Think things that make you happy with you, or just connect to your breath and feel how each inhale gives strength to all parts of your body. Feel grateful for that.

3. Write minimum three compliments to yourself that make you feel proud to be you: put them up on your bathroom mirror and read them every day when you brush your teeth.

4. Think about the negative things you tell yourself: notice every time you say, "I can't", "I'm not good enough" or "that person is better than me" and stop. Then reverse it in your head and say "I can!", "I am good enough", "I am better at being me than anyone in this whole world will ever be". Think about it, how fucking cool is that?

MAYA KIUSALAAS

HELP!

My diary -14 years old

"Now I have been going to Mia for a couple of months for my eating disorders, or is it anorexia? It's a lot of things you don't know. Haha. Mia is a wonderful human I will cherish for the rest of my life. We talk about everything one can possibly talk about! Things like: Who am I? What is the meaning of life?

My eating disorders come from problems that I am not aware of yet. They are like "the tip of an iceberg". The only visible problem, the dot above the i. On the first appointment; we compared my situation to a captain who was crossing the sea full of stones and shallow waters, with a broken compass. That was clever! Because that is exactly how I feel"

I hadn't been as strict as the bullies in my head wanted me to be. I had put up a million rules about how to eat and not to eat and I had not always been able to follow them (because they were impossible to live by). Breaking the rules meant that those horrible voices inside my head were screaming loud at me – telling me what a useless, ugly person I was. I had eaten more than I believed I was worth and I punished myself for it.

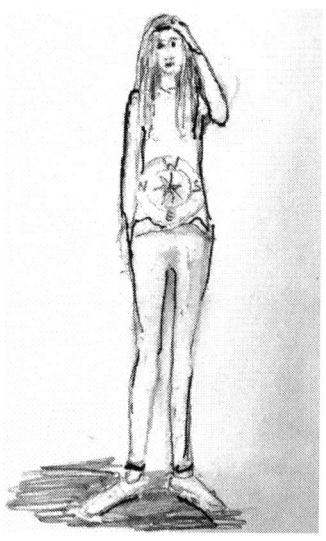

I didn't know what to do. I wanted to just turn my skin inside out. I think the only thing I can describe it as, is panic. I had panic, I was panic, and I didn't know what to do with my emotions and myself. They were overwhelming. My nails scratched my skin like I had to dig somebody out of there. FUCK FUCK FUCK FUCK. I felt like I could projectile it all out. I screamed out loud, stamped my feet and punched myself in the face. A million voices tried to tell me what to do. I didn't know how to express my emotions. I knew that they were all unhelpful, but they were all I had to live with. I didn't know how to invite the good voices and emotions in, not yet. The emotions I had didn't fit, I had no reason to be so angry, but I was. I needed help to sort myself out.

Mia Andersson's office was on the eleventh floor in Fridhemsplan in central Stockholm. I always walked up all the stairs. A month before I went in for my first talk with her and her fifty-year-old "intern" Per, I had made sure not to eat anything so that I could fit in in the waiting room at the Anorexia and Bulimia Clinic she ran. In hindsight, all that starvation was wasted. I went there for over a year and I only shared the waiting room with somebody once, but I needed to justify to myself and to others that I was worthy of her time.

Mia and Per turned out to be my absolute safest place in this world. The only place where I thought it all made sense. In that room, we never mentioned food or what is "normal" to eat. They never talked about anorexia as an eating disorder; they knew that it is a self-love disorder that makes you feel so lost in this world that you just focus on creating some kind of order for yourself. I thought by changing myself through starvation, I could make me love myself, but all it did was make me feel more lost, more obsessed and feel less love for myself. But by then I had no idea how to separate myself from the disease; it had become a part of me.

"The dangerous thing is that I really enjoy the attention I get. What will happen if / when everything is ok? Will I cease to exist?

I wonder if people lie when they say that I don't look bloated?! I have skinny arms and sort of skinny legs (SORT OF) but I DON'T think that my stomach is skinny. Mia showed me a picture that she had in her room, on the wall. It showed three stages. There was a casket, a skeleton with a ball and chain and then a girl with an orange dress jumping barefoot on a grass field. She asked me which one I could relate to; I answered the middle one. I am an insignificant human, and I am empty, stuck and if you pour anything into it- it would just slip right through. Then she asked me if I could ever see myself as that girl dancing barefoot in a dress with a tulip in her hand. She asked if I thought that I could ever be happy, excited and content with life and who I am. Honestly, I answered; no. A black tunnel without an end. "

MAYA KIUSALAAS

"My Anorexic dream"
I want to be happy with my body
I want attention.
I want people to see me.
I want people to think that I am beautiful.
I don't want people to just see my friends when we walk on the street.
I want to be enough for other people.
I want to be able to walk without covering my stomach.

"Negative with Anorexia"
I feel trapped, tied up, locked in. Sad.
I feel so trapped and controlled/controlling
I am so obsessed with food. It's not fun. I want it but I can't have it.
When I eat, I cannot stop.
As soon as I eat I get sad, panic and depressed, I have to work out so that I will not get fat.

-14 years old

Hot Tip

I should've written a list of the positives of not being obsessed. I needed then to envision a life without being locked in instead of just comparing one negative to another. My two scenarios were sick or panic; I needed another dream. I needed a happy vision full of love and I didn't know that it was in my own hands to create that reality for myself. Yet.

The key to being well and healthy is to visualize (and feel) your life as you would love to live it.

If I could go back I would create a vision where I was free, happy excited about life and myself. I would see where I wanted to be. If I had of thought about it, and focused on that then I would've figured out how to get there. Instead, I focused on what I was scared of, and the shit I was living with. ***Our brains create what we put attention towards.*** *I know that now, and I wish someone could've made me understand that then.*

Today, if I feel sad, anxious or if I feel as if I have lost the love for myself and this world I sit down and ask myself to write down everything that I do love about myself, I make myself feel pride and excitement. I create my dream world in which I am free, full of confidence and self-love. I visualize myself walking the streets with my head up high, smiling out of love to every person that I meet. I connect to the place inside of me where love is all there is and I feel that for myself. I shift the focus from what I don't have to what I do have and find a trust in myself that I am good enough just the way I am. If I am not happy, I know that I need to change the way I look at things, not myself. I know that when I start looking for what I want to do, what makes me happy and act with a purpose of being as much of myself as I can possibly be, then I have opened up a door into life itself. I just need to connect to my true emotions and stop living and listening to the voices in my head.

For me to be able to be free, I needed to imagine what life would be like if I was free. I would've written:

"Positives with being free"
I am able to listen to my body and look after it with love.
I live a life where I am excited to live, play, laugh, feel and love.
I love myself as I love all my friends, and I know that they love me just the way I am.
The only person I try to be like is myself.
I know what I love to do and I do it because I like doing it.
I choose not to do things that make me feel uncomfortable.
I choose to do things that I feel comfortable doing.
I feel strong because I see and trust that I can always choose.
I am surrounded by people who love me.
I am good enough the way I am.
I am unique and loving.
I am proud to be me and confident to express myself.
I don't care about what other people think of me because I will not change who I truly am anyway.

Action:

1. Grab a pen and paper and put the timer on for five minutes. Write down everything that you dream of in life, anything, from good emotions you want to last, to things that you want for your life and future.

2. Write a story about yourself where you pretend that you have everything that you just wrote down: focus on how you would feel in this story (remember; nothing is impossible, no dreams are too big – if you dream about bringing all of your friends and family for a holiday to Mars you can).

3. Understand that whatever you want to do and work towards – you can! The only limitations are in your own mind. Get rid of the limitations and anything is possible: you are limitless

How do you get rid of the limitations?

You have to understand and believe that you create your own limitations in your head. What is stopping you from doing what you really want to do? Unless what you are really dreaming of doing includes breaking the laws there are ways to achieve anything. The question is "how much time are you willing to spend on this?"

MAYA KIUSALAAS

THE LUNCH GROUP

I went to a government-run eating disorder centre at one stage. It was called "The Lunch Group". It might as well have been called "what an average person eats". We got shown pictures of what a "normal" lunch looked like and got an hour of food talk. Later we were dragged down to a greasy pub for lunch. We were a quite chatty group of girls despite our emotional baggage, but when we were forced to eat, we all hated the world – we became victims of it. If we didn't finish the lunch we ordered; we had to drink nutrition shakes to get "the right amount of calories".

They took away our only surviving mechanism; Control. We weren't allowed to use the toilet for 30 minutes after lunch, but sometimes we managed to run to the toilet without the doctors or nutritionists catching us. It was horrible when I think about it. Horrible because they actually had no idea what they were doing even though they meant well. Mia knew this. She knew that all they need to focus on is self-love and value.

"When I started year nine, so many people said, "Finally, you have put on some kilos and feel better than last year".

Thanks for that, I thought, and started to starve again. Before The Lunch Group every Wednesday my situation went up and down like an uncontrollable roller coaster. Still obsessed with food, but now the opposite. Binge-starve-binge-starve. The Lunch Group changed everything. I felt a pressure, again, that I needed to be skinny to be accepted there. I think people want (but still don't want?) me to be skinny, I mean who am I if I am not? Will nobody notice me if I am not?

At the end of the summer (of year 8) I experienced the wonderful world of food, and it was hard to go back to starve myself again. I learnt how to vomit. It is horrible! I could throw up so many times during one day. In secret. I snuck in plastic bags into my room, in a little tin jar. There it could be three filled bags for days before I got the chance to throw them out without people noticing. I often vomited in the shower. It got clogged up a lot. The toilet is best, but people notice that. I haven't eaten almost anything for five weeks, but three days ago I decided that I have to put an end to this. I have started to eat normally, and I fight not to overeat on each meal, so far so good. I hope I can handle a weight gain again. I am a little scared, but it feels good. I have energy. Tomorrow I will shine at The

Lunch Group. I have never managed to finish a whole meal there… but tomorrow I will. 🥣"

- 15 years old.

Hot Tip

If you are dealing with any sort of eating disorder at present or if you are obsessing in any way about your body image or if you don't love the person you are now and think that you have to change:

*I am telling you now to **tell all the voices in your head to shut the fuck up**. Start telling them that every time you notice them.*

*And **start writing lists, letters and paint out pictures of who you really want to be, and what you do love about yourself. Start feeling (or pretend to feel if you can't find the emotions yet) that you care about yourself like you would care for a friend you love**. If you push yourself too hard, ask yourself if you would push your friend that hard? **Stop judging yourself and try to feel what you feel for others for yourself.***

If you want freedom and love, you have to find a way to connect with your inner freedom and love to yourself. Writing positive lists and letters to myself made me see more and more things about myself that I loved, and slowly I could build up a confidence that allowed me to feel free, happy and loved. Meditation and yoga are also good tools to use to focus on self-love and healing. If you are feeling really overwhelmed I would always encourage that you seek professional help. You may not find the right counsellor, psychologist, nutritionist or GP on the first go, but professionals can really make a difference in your recovery. Keep asking for help until you find the person who gets what you are going through.

*The sooner you start fighting the negative voices in your head, the better. Even if you believe they are telling the truth **(they are not)**, fight them anyway. Because they are trying to prevent you from living your life, and what is the meaning of life? To be lived. So that is why those inner critics are just idiots. They are working against life. As soon as you realise that they are in your head and you can figure out how to live with your heart and soul, find the love within, the voices will lose their power over your life. When you stop listening to them, they will start listening to the **you** that lives through love.*

Action:

1. Write yourself a letter, pretending that you are your own best friend. In the letter include;

why you think that you are such a good friend, what makes it fun being around you, something nice that you often do for others, what people get inspired by when they are around you. Keep that letter nearby and read it every day, it will remind you that you are a good friend to yourself and to others!

2. All the emotions you have will teach you something. Write down all emotions that you can feel and what they can teach you.

e.g. **Sadness** will teach me how much I appreciate happiness and it will also teach me to feel for others when they are sad so that maybe I can help them.

Anger teaches me that I care for something I can't find words to express, once I learn how to communicate my anger through writing, words, paintings, poems, songs I can help myself and what I care for.

Anxiety and **Depression** teach me to listen to my body and my emotions and communicate with my soul, what is my inside trying to communicate to me?

Happiness teaches me that there is no better feeling than laughing (so much my stomach hurts.)

Now it's your turn!

P.S.   Remember that you don't have to do this on your own. Help is available to you.

MAYA KIUSALAAS

THE BLACK SHEEP

I had created a story for myself and I chose to believe it – live up to it. I kept saying that I was the black sheep of my family, that I didn't have any creativity inside of me and that I didn't have any hobbies. So, obviously, I couldn't be creative or fit in or have hobbies, I wouldn't let myself. I collected evidence to prove my point and I lived my life wondering how my life would pan out, without interests. I went to the gym every day, but I didn't enjoy it. I worked out hard, but I wasn't inspired. I loved when it was over. That was what I strived for. "Please make time fly at the gym so that I can tick this off my list and feel good about myself." My only goal was to look skinny. I wished I would've valued happiness higher; life would've been so much more fun if I valued fun.

I described and saw myself as a healthy person, I never ate carbs or actual sugar, but there was nothing healthy about the way I lived. Once I stopped starving myself it showed in the way I looked, but more importantly, the way I felt. The chemicals in my food and drink seriously affect my emotional chemistry.

FREE THE GIRL

Once I stopped eating chemicals; artificial sugars, alcohol, processed food, preservatives, hormones in dairy and meat and all the other un-natural things on the shelf, I felt so much better both mentally and physically.

Guilt was a feeling that plagued my body more often than not. I felt constantly guilty. Guilty for eating, guilty for not eating, guilty for being a sloth on the couch, guilty for drinking too much, fear of missing out when I didn't go out. There was vomiting, there was anxiety, there was frustration, and there was a scream for love and fulfilment. The black hole of my young adult years; the emptiness of self-love.

I had friends, and I had a fun life. I loved my school, loved to be social but at the same time, I've never felt good enough for my friends. In high school, I felt as if I was constantly being judged, almost like in an American high school movie. I always felt like I didn't belong there. I wasn't good enough for them unless I changed who I was, that's how I felt... But maybe I didn't think that I was good enough for anyone? Maybe I could've been a part of any group and still feel the same emotions of being wrong. I made myself feel this way because my confidence was non-excitant. I let myself be pushed around. All I wanted was to feel safe and loved, but I probably did what most insecure young girls do; Try to change in order to fit in. The thing is that I never knew then that my confidence was bad. I could always speak to anyone and everyone, I was loud and noisy in school, but I saw myself like I was worth less than everyone around me.

I was angry, frustrated with so many things in my life. Why couldn't I be like them? Why wasn't I as good looking as them? Why didn't people like me as much? Why did I have anxiety? Why did I hate my body and myself? Why couldn't I just live happily and with a calm mind? What would my life turn out to be? Would I ever learn to love myself? Will I hate myself for the rest of my life? Will I be alone for the rest of my life? Do people hate me? Who would cry at my funeral?

Hot Tip

I wished I could have understood that I can be friends with everyone. It is up to me to find the confidence to choose who I want to talk to or be with. I can be part of many groups and circles and communities. If I had more confidence and understood my core values I would have understood that I can be whoever I want to be and people can either take it or leave it. I would've understood that I'm not required to change who I am and how I behave around people in order to gain anyone's approval.

Action:

1. Write down as many people as you know whom you feel comfortable being around! Why do you think that you are able to feel comfortable around them? Is it because of the way they act or is it because of the way you feel around them?

2. Write down of a couple of people who you feel more pressure to behave in a certain way when you are around them? Why do you think that you feel pressure to act a certain way around them?

3. Write down three things that you can do to feel and connect and be comfortable and confident the next time you are around people who "make you feel" pressured.

e.g. think of your friends who you feel comfortable to be around, how would you act around them? Find the confidence and strength inside your body and mind through three deep belly breaths or through drumming on your chest like a gorilla. Find the confident person inside of you and have your confidence sit on your shoulder and support you by reminding you of who you really are!

Remember that you **never** have to act in any special way, ever, you always have a choice! The more you practice, the more relaxed and confident you will feel!

(If possible, spend more time with the people who you feel comfortable being around!)

LOOKING BACK

Today I am grateful for anorexia, body obsession, anxiety, and depression. I am grateful for feeling lonely and lost, and if I could change anything, it wouldn't be much. I can relate to so much more in life because of it, and that is one of life's greatest gifts. Feeling down, lost and scared has also given me the gift of being able to also feel extremely, explosively happy and excited. It means that, for me, I can appreciate happiness so much more than I would've been able to if I hadn't experienced the black holes that I have been in. I am proud that I kept searching, hunting for truth and happiness. I am grateful because feeling bad made me ask the right questions so that I could learn how to feel amazing.

I'm writing this book for myself; I'm not going to lie. I'm writing it because I fucking love trying to figure out why I've done things that I've done and why I've felt things that I've felt about stuff. It used to be my whole life, this stuff, it is now nothing more than a memory to me. I love figuring myself out and also trying to figure out how I act in different groups of people, all the time still being true to who I am. I also love writing this to share it with other people because maybe it opens up things that they otherwise mightn't have been able to feel. Hopefully, I can share this so that you can realise that you don't have to fit in in any group that makes you feel like you are wrong. I write this for myself with a dream that I can free some people from trying to be somebody that, deep down, they don't want to be, but think that they have to be. I do that because that person was me some time ago. It is time to connect to who we really are and want to be in this world and don't let anyone blow that candle out.

What I understand today, many people have told me before. People have told me how to act, think and be. They have told me what I should be happy for and what I should change, and I am grateful for everything people have done for me and asked me to see. But I realise now that I had to understand this for myself, on an emotional level, through my own experiences, and I had to go through all of the steps and learn all of the lessons I have learnt in order to fully understand what it means to be free.

So do what you have to do. Go on your journey, just know there is ALWAYS, always a choice and always a way back home. No matter where you are or how lost you feel. Always.

Hot Tip

Sometimes our hardest battles are what gives us our unique powers. We can either let experiences defeat us – just let the bad experiences decide that the rest of our lives will be as shit, or we can get angry at whatever happened to us but then decide that even though something shit happened to us we will not let that decide for us that the rest of our lives will be shit because of it. Instead we can extract everything that can make us to a stronger and wiser person and use our struggles as a way of connecting and relating to other humans or use them as hidden super powers (sometimes it can feel quite cool to know that you have experienced a complicated and hard emotion/situation – and survived it! Use it to find confidence).

Action:

1. Think about a mistake you have made in the past, or something hard you have had to go through emotionally, that has helped you understand the world in a new way? What would your world look like if you had never been through that?

2. If you still wish you never had to go through it, write down three things that you learnt from it anyway, even if it is hard.

SECTION 4

BULIMIA – THE CURSE

This chapter deals with thoughts about bulimia and how to break free from it.

MAYA KIUSALAAS

MOST OF THE HORROR I WILL SPARE YOU

I have always loved my own gravity towards being open with my emotions, and honest with my thoughts. I have loved and valued (and still do) my lack of fear for saying out loud what I am thinking. But by being so open and honest with the world, I thought that the brain voices, the ones that appear to be my thoughts, always told me the truth, but I couldn't have been more wrong. The brain voices are scared. They live in the past and worry about the future, so that's where I was living. I was never here in the present, aware of the now. My brain was always somewhere else, never actually living life as it unfolded. That meant my body could never connect to me, I was just connected to my guilt in the past and my worries about the future. I felt like there wasn't anything wrong with me, I was wrong. I was filled with so much anger and frustration, it had become everything by then. It was explosive, and I couldn't figure out how to control it.

The year of anorexia came to an end when I learned how to vomit- the most self-destructing lesson I've taught myself, in my life. It was worse than everything I had ever experienced, but I allowed myself to continue – I was addicted. I was on a strict diet, which meant that I basically did not eat. Until I was alone. Then I ate everything. While I was cooking pasta, oats and toast, I ate chips and ice-cream straight out of the package. I didn't even bother to swallow the pasta before I shoved the ice-cream in my mouth. If you saw me I would've looked possessed, and in a way I was. I devoured everything my conscious normally couldn't bear and then I went to the toilet and flushed it down with all the guilt. Back to the kitchen I went and did it all over again. Maybe five or six times or until someone got home... my throat was burning; my self-respect was non-existent. I saw myself in the mirror, with bloodshot eyes, a swollen face and thought that if anyone knew, they would look at me and think that I am the most disgusting person in the world.

If there is anything I wish I had never done it is starting to throw up. And I really want to scare everyone who reads this away from ever trying to explore it. There are a lot of things that I believe that every person might have to go through to grow as a person. I believe in mistakes and I think that it is valuable for all of us to make them – so that we can learn from them. But this "mistake" of mine caused so much panic, problems, stress, anxiety, guilt, sadness, pain and loss of self-respect and love that **I simply beg to all people out there not to experiment with this**. Let my pain speak for you. Going down this rabbit hole will never make you feel love and excitement for yourself; take my word for it. If you or someone you know is thinking about engaging in this behaviour then I would encourage you to seek help, from a friend, family member, a teacher, school counsellor or anyone you feel safe with – fight it with every strong cell in your body.

It is like being nauseous, but not with nausea, with just control, panic, guilt and anxiety. It's a trap that only you yourself can save you from. The more we do things, the less "weird" they become. But instead of you just start to feel comfortable with yourself doing it – you get more and more uncomfortable with yourself yet more and more trapped with your behaviour pattern.

You might think (and feel) as if vomiting it is a solution as long as you can keep it a secret with yourself. Maybe you believe that it will keep you safe from those mean and horrible thoughts in your head that make you believe that you need to change how you look and who you are to be loved. I promise you that even if you believe that it is a solution, it is not. YOU need to be aware when those thoughts arise in your mind and when they do you need to take a deep breath and choose to go with health, love, happiness and freedom – that's the only solution. Make a statement every time you choose not to listen to them, and give yourself a big fat proud smile. Every time you choose not to vomit YOU have won!

No, there was nothing pretty about vomiting. It was a curse that could only be broken by creating some respect for myself. It is a distraction from life itself because it absorbs all your time and energy. At least it did for me. I wish I would've just started to meditate and try to connect to my own body instead of completely shut it out and distance myself from it. But…

Six years went past. And like seasons bulimia came and went, but my confidence was always absent. It wasn't until I started to care about my body and its health for real, and tried to actually feel good that I could stop throwing up. I believe now that if I would've learnt how to **meditate** and **treat food as nutrition and medicine** rather than a filling mechanism I would've been able to stop my vomiting earlier. I don't think that I fully grasped the fact that **food is the source of life** and the **gateway to health**; I only saw what would make me fat. I didn't understand what part the food plays in creating good chemical reactions in our body and how you can heal through the right nutrition.

Bulimia is a hard nut to crack. There are so many internal forces that are fighting with each other. Hunger, control, guilt, beauty, comparison, lack of self-love and respect. Bulimia is also so different depending on the person who experiences it, but it is all linked together with a feeling of guilt connected to eating.

No-one with self-respect and love would ever do that to their body and mind. That is a fact. Rather than teaching girls with bulimia and anorexia how to eat we have to create a system that can help girls love and respect themselves and their bodies. Today's society is too corrupt when it comes to diet and nutrition, but there are many good knowledgeable doctors and psychiatrists out there too, you just have to have patience finding someone that you feel that you can trust. Most important of all, **eating disorders have almost nothing to do with food**, so we have to avoid treating it with food plans and lessons about "normal" eating habits. **We have to start treating it with love.**

If you have a person you can speak with about this, you can even talk to them when the guilt kicks in and just let them know that right now you are fighting with guilt, anxiety or whatever other feeling that might trigger you to throw up. When you let that fear out in the light and when you fight it and let someone know that you won – that used to be a very good feeling for me!

(If you don't have a person you feel like talking to you can find one through a help line, a nurse in school, a supportive person online or even a friend you make up in your mind – your own support team!)

The only thing that helped me when it came to throwing up was telling the people who were closest to me about it. I told my parents, even though I felt like hiding it from them was my security guard that kept my control intact. I felt like if I told them I would cut off all of my safety-lines and start falling deep into a black hole. It was hard even thinking about telling them, but once I had told them it didn't feel scary or hard at all. It felt the opposite of falling, instead, it felt like someone was lifting me up – like I had support. I felt free! I also told my best friends, only so I wouldn't be tempted to throw up around them. Even that wasn't as scary as I had predicted in my head. I thought that I would panic from losing the control, but freedom was all I felt. I finally felt that I had taken real control over my freedom.

The control I believed that I had inside my secret turned out to be fake. With my secret life of throwing up, I felt like I was in charge, like I could handle my feelings of guilt. It turned out that once the people around me knew, I felt more in control than I had in a long time and the control wasn't mixed with guilt, shame and panic; it was mixed with love, trust and freedom. No matter how hard it felt to tell people my secret – the moment I did I never regretted it a bit (half of the people that I told already suspected that that was the case anyway – they knew more than I believed that they knew!)

Hot Tip

If I was that girl still, I wish someone could've made me try this and make me really invest my emotions in it:

Tune into your actual emotions and listen to which emotions are actually there.

Example: emotions I used to feel back then were: stress from not knowing who I was and what I wanted and for not being perfect, scared to lose control, guilt for not doing things right, fear of being forgotten, extreme need to be happy and loved, always thinking about the next step, never present in the moment.

Action:

1. Write the emotions you wish to live without down on a piece of paper and burn it in a fireplace, ship it off to sea in a glass bottle, tare it up into a million pieces and throw it in a bin; make a statement to yourself and your brain showing it that you will not take the shit anymore.

   You might think that the negative voices in your head are telling you the truth, they aren't. They are just your brain voices, your inner critic's voices, you are not your thoughts. The truth is that you should do the things you love and be the person who you feel comfortable being. That person accepts you for just being you.

2. **What does your body actually need?** One thing that we need to understand is the fact that today's food culture is mostly based around money. All food companies want people to think that the more you eat of certain products- the better you will feel. Why? Because then you buy more. For so long I thought that I had to eat six small meals a day or I'll get fat and crash!

It wasn't until **I stopped being so focused on what other people told me to do and instead started to listen to my actual hunger** I found this calm relation to food. **I stopped thinking of food in combination with timing and weight and I started to treat food as medicine**; to provide my body with all the amazing nutrition it needs. Your body tells you when it is hungry, listen. (good food choices are suggested in the next step).

3. **Stop aiming to lose weight.** Once I stopped thinking about food as a weight loss tool, and

once my goal with my body went from being skinny and beautiful to **feeling amazing**, my body just took the shape I've always wanted.

I stopped obsessing and stressing about looks and started to do things to actually feel good and be able to **live**. I make sure that I research what food is best for my body, and really, if we all start listening to our bodies needs, we will quickly find that **natural**, and **non-processed food**, makes our bodies happy. I eat a lot of raw vegetables and fresh produce so if I sometimes feel like something 'cheeky' or less healthy I know that I can eat it without interrupting my inner balance too much. The majority of the time I eat what will nourish and fuel my body because my goal is to feel amazing all the time. I know that I will never start eating crap food on a regular basis anyway because that would be neglecting my body's actual needs, and not supporting my happy emotions or my love for myself.

MAYA KIUSALAAS

WHAT IF MY FRIEND IS STRUGGLING?

As a teenager with an already broken self-image and confidence, I found it hard to listen when my friends talked about looks and weight. I always compared myself with my friends. I compared myself with everybody, and in my head, I always considered myself less beautiful and less worthy. When they talked down to themselves I took it as a direct attack on me. If someone said, "I am fat", it was like they had said to me that I needed to change my looks or they wouldn't be my friend. Extreme and crazy, I know, but that is what my inner critics turned it into – and I chose to listen to them because I didn't know that they were full of shit, yet. See, the inner critics are super egoistic, they want you to believe that everything has everything to do with you – but it doesn't.

You know how you look at your friends; you see only what is good about them, and if you see flaws with them you accept them and like them, sometimes even more, for the flaws too, right? You would never use the same magnifying glass you use on yourself to find and point out everything that isn't ideal with them. Everybody is too obsessed about their own shit, they don't have time to think about that little pimple on your forehead, only you care, when you are standing five centimetres from the bathroom mirror. I also understand now that I can never blame or judge anyone for how they act or know what they are struggling with – everyone is going through their own shit and trying to work out how to live in their world.

I can't say that it was my friend's fault that I looked down on myself at all, because it wasn't. I can't say, "because they didn't or did like themselves, I didn't like myself and if they would've changed I would've felt different about myself", that is just shifting the blame. What I felt had nothing to do with what my friends was really doing. As long as you blame your shit on other people you will not be able to see what changes YOU need to make in order to feel better about yourself and your situation. My friends weren't the voices in my head, and they never told me to listen to those voices either, but I did it anyway. I take full responsibility for my actions, I have to, or else I will never change my reality. I made those choices to hear it that way, to believe the stuff in my head.

It is so hard to catch yourself blaming people and circumstances because we do it without thinking about it. I think that I still do it sometimes – but I try to see when I am doing it and stop because change in life never comes from shifting the blame from you to them, it comes from the decision of accepting that something is the way it is and choosing to move forward from that point – no matter what happened.

If I suspected that one of my friends was keeping secrets about their relationship with food it made me feel stressed. What if they knew how to diet and be skinny and more beautiful and they wouldn't share it with me? It made me feel like I was behind and I had to get in on the secret. The critics in my head told me that I had to struggle the most out of every one of my friends. I didn't realise that only made things worse. Why? Because now I struggled more and my friends started to find it stressful to be around me. Think about it; who would you like to have around you? Someone who is constantly stressed, anxious and lacking the confidence to take care of themselves or someone who is living life happily and being truthful with who they are and what they are doing?

You have a choice. In situations where you feel that your friends are making choices that impact you in a stressful, fearful or negative way, you can choose to do what you know, deep inside, is the right thing to do.

Ask yourself "Is this a step towards a sustainable lifestyle?"

In the end, you have to make this choice alone and hope that as many of your friends follow if you choose to put your focus and energy towards doing what makes you happy, healthy and full of love– because you can never change anyone by telling them what to do, you can only do what you are doing and let people know why you are doing what you are doing. If you are being truthful to yourself and look after your inside and outside with as much love and nurture as possible, your friends will see that what you are doing is working – because the inside always shines through!

This isn't just for eating restrictions. You can make your own choices about anything. Just because your friend might be drinking, or smoking, doing drugs, stealing or bullying, you don't have to make their choices your own.

If someone is doing something that doesn't sit right with you; do something that does feel right to you instead. That might be just to leave the conversation, go and hang out with someone else for a while – just take a break, or maybe if the person is mean to someone else the right thing for you to do might be to tell your friend how awkward it makes you feel when he/she is doing that to another person. There are millions of possible things to do in a situation where you don't feel quite right; you have just got to ask yourself what that might be and then do it! It gets easier and easier every time you step up for yourself! Your friends will respect you more for it and you set yourself up for a life of happiness and fulfilment every time you follow what you know is right, you win.

Hot Tip

Being around friends who make the "wrong" choices without letting them affect you is only hard if you're not fully confident in who you are and why you are doing what you are doing. You need to ask yourself WHY you would follow a trend. Why should you do what they are doing and what does that make you?

If you see that your friend is struggling and you are worried, ask him/her how they are feeling (really feeling). Don't take the responsibility to try to help them all alone! If you feel safe, share some things that you have done to make you feel better with yourself and your relationship with your body. It is also good to share with them any adults who have helped you; the local GP, school nurse, helpline, psychologist etc.

Action:

If someone is talking down to themselves in front of you, it usually means that they are insecure and want you to tell them that what they are saying isn't true. Instead of doing that:

1. Ask them to say three things that they like about themselves.
   In getting your friends to tell them good thing about themselves you are helping them to understand and feel good things rather than feeding a negative habit.

2. If someone says something you don't agree with, rather than disagree, ask them why they think that. Usually, it's only the illogical shit in

their head saying this stupid stuff. As soon as you ask them to be logical about it, they realise it's pretty stupid. It's fake. It's not real. i.e. if someone says to you, "Nothing ever goes my way." Or, "Everybody hates me", you can just say, "Really? Nothing EVER goes your way, I bet you can tell me at least two times when something did go your way?" and they will start to think of times when things did go okay (because of course they sometimes do) or you say, "Really NO ONE likes you. If you think about it I think that you can come up with minimum five people who love the shit out of you – I am one of them!" and they will start to think of more people who do like them. Or if they say, "That person hates me." You can say, "How do you know they hate you?" and they will list some things and it's easy to see that maybe that's not hate, maybe it's something else.

3. Start a game where you and your friends together answer the question "What is the best thing about our friend group or with us as friends". Get them in on the secret that

loving yourself and who you are is a miracle. It makes you smile a lot more than talking about what is negative with you or the people around you.

4. When we lose touch with who we are and what we have to be grateful for we might start to compare ourselves with others; friends, celebrities or random people on the street. We tend to see the beauty and happiness in their life and instantly think that if we were them, or more like them, we will be happy. Happiness, confidence, self-love and excitement is nowhere to be found in the land of comparing. EVER.

Next time you find yourself dreaming about being more like someone else or have what they've got – think about five, ten or fifty things within you, your life and the world around you that YOU have to be grateful for and don't waste any time swimming around in that black hole. You don't ever know what journey someone else is on. This is your journey, only you can complete it, which means that what you have to love and connect to is all there inside of you!

GO FIND IT – and be proud!

SECTION 5

KNOW YOUR BODY

What you eat (or don't eat) can have a large effect on the way you feel, the amount of motivation you have, even the way you behave. I am not an expert in diet or nutrition, so I shouldn't be the ultimate source for your knowledge about nutrition. I will mention a couple of experts in this book that you can look into if this subject speaks to you. But I do find it fascinating and I know that what and how I eat affects how I feel both mentally and physically.

In the sections about food I ask you to just consider how the food you eat possibly affects you. I encourage you to try a few things out and see if they make you feel different. Listen to the signals your body are sending you and learn to feel what sits right with you – and do your own research. Nutrition and diet is an evolving subject so what is "right" today might have changed tomorrow!

THE UNIVERSE INSIDE OF US

Did you know that there are studies, done at McMaster University in Hamilton, presented in Giulia Enders Book *GUT – the inside story of our body's most under-rated organ*, where they swapped the gut bacteria in mice (we have gut bacteria too, it's mainly in our large intestine) with different mice who had different behaviour patterns, and the mice started behaving differently, they swapped actions over! Other studies also show that when human start looking after their diet (reducing sugar and avoiding refined carbs such as white bread and white rice) and focussed on eating good fibre from a variety of vegetables their behaviour change too. They felt happier and more motivated.

If you need more tips and guidance to learn more about how to look after your body, look at people such as **Kelly Brogan** and listen to what she has to say about food and how your food affects your whole well-being.

TRY IT OUT!

1. Swap out all white bread, white rice and white pasta to whole grain options (try gluten free) for a month.

2. Get rid of all sugary soft drinks or diet alternatives, fruit juices and drink just water, green tea or kombucha for a month. (kombucha is fermented tea with natural flavour)

3. Write down possible changes in your mood and energy levels that you see when trying different foods. 20 minutes after you eat write down how you are feeling. See if you can find a connection to your mood or energy levels and what you eat. If you aren't eating (hopefully you are) pay attention to how starving yourself feels. Are you cold, get sick all the time, have no energy, no or interrupted menstrual cycle, irritable, anxious, lose focus quickly, can't remember things or understand simple concepts? Get to understand that these are related to not eating. Find foods that will

sustain you over a long period of time, not a quick fix that's high in refined carbs and sugar that will have you feeling worse than before as soon as the sugar high drops.

4. Work out with love and listen to your body. Stop working out with a goal of trying to change your body or justify eating food. I used to work out to lose weight. I worked out to be able to eat. Once I realised that that didn't make me feel good, happy, nor was it the best for my body and I started to work out when my body felt like it because I know that it is making my body happy, healthy and energised.

Once I stopped stressing and started to rest and just move naturally, my body finally felt like a home to me. I went from waking up at 5am every morning, (even on holidays), to work out just to justify eating food, to working out only if I feel like it. For the first time in what feels like forever, I am actually happy and proud of my body.

If anyone would've told me to rest back then I would've thought that it would equal me feeling like a fat, soggy, blob. I realised that it is the stress about getting enough exercise, eating less and constantly burning calories that made me feel puffy. When I stopped stressing my body finally found harmony, I looked better and felt better.

Every time I hear my brain telling me to work out with the motivation to either lose weight, change my body shape or burn calories I fight it, even when it's hard. I only listen to my body when it tells me to work out because I want to feel that endorphin rush or if my legs feel like running or I just genuinely want to lift some weights. I work out to feel amazing, not to please my inner critic.

Take one step at the time and always listen to your emotions. It might feel overwhelming but just start with one good thing, and then, once you feel comfortable, move on to the next thing.

I understand that this might be hard for you to take in and believe if you are already deeply invested in your lack of self-love. I know that if somebody would have told me this when I was so empty of self-love and so obsessed with whatever I was obsessed with at the time, I would have doubted it. I also know that I would try anything that could help me feel happy. When I was "sick" I didn't think that I wanted to be well, because I thought that well meant fat and unhappy (that is actually what I believed. Now I know that that is so far away from what well means that it is almost ridiculous). I know now that that is not a definition of well. The problem was that I had nothing to compare it with. I didn't know then that **well and happy means happy with everything about you and self-love actually can mean to love yourself like you love someone else**.

You have to create a life for yourself that you want to believe is true. Imagine and feel yourself loving you so much that you want to bounce up and down out of excitement. Well means to be free from being ruled by the fear of not being good enough and free from fear of being judged. Imagine feeling, "FUCK YES" when you think about all the beautiful things with yourself and feeling free to express everything that you are with pride. That is to feel well.

Hot Tip

*Once I started to figure out who I wanted to be rather who I didn't want to be, I started to explore the opportunities I had in life – I didn't have to change who I was in order to deserve love. And once I started realising that fake food, like diet coke and shit, didn't make me feel better and I started to **eat for nutrition and healing my body;** I noticed that I felt better (try it and see for yourself). Then I started to listen to my body's hunger, and I felt even better. And then I started not to push my body so hard and valued relaxation too, and I have never felt better with my body. I trust that my body will take me where I want to go if I listen, let it and give it the best possible chance to do so. The way that I feel by just listening to my body is amazing. I actually feel amazing, you can too!*

Action:

1. Before you eat something, sit down and take ten deep-deep breaths. Find a calm inside your body and mind.

2. Make sure that what you eat will bring nutrition, vitamins, minerals and fibres into your gut, and calm to your brain **by choosing natural fruit, vegetables, nuts, beans, and fresh meat.**

3. If you would ever feel guilt in relationship to food; it is your mind's way of signalling to you that you need to find a new approach and relationship to food and nutrition. Sit down, preferably at least an hour before your next meal, and write down what you want to get out of:
a) your body
b) your food

e.g. a) My body is an extension of my mind and soul. My body can walk, run, jump and express all sorts of emotions. I love waking up feeling energized in all of my cells; from my toes to my hair. **I want my body to support me so that I can feel strong, confident and relaxed all the time.** I want to be able to communicate with my body so that I know what it needs to give me the excitement I want in and of life.

b) I want to eat what tastes good and satisfies me. I want it to travel down in my gut and from there spread out to the rest of my body to help it generate energy **to heal, build and energize**. I want to feel full and satisfied and I want my body to have everything that it needs to make me happy and full of life.

4. Write down a list of ten small (or big) changes you can make in your life right now that will make you a little bit happier.

e.g. 1. Put my alarm on ten minutes before I need to get out of bed and use that time to feel how my body is feeling, listen to if there is anything it might try to tell me. 2. Say some nice things to my body and mind, 3. Finish my shower on cold (or shower cold the whole time) to wake up every cell in my body. 4. Meditate for 5 – 10 minutes before school. 5. Listen to a song that makes me feel happy. 6. Make sure I get at least 20 minutes of natural sunlight per day. 7. Take ten deep calming breaths. 8. Call a friend. 9. Paint. 10. Write down ten things that make you feel love…

Now it's your turn!

GUT HEALTH

There are a lot of good doctors and scientists out there who talk about how natural food affects your mood and psychological health. They can explain it much better than I can but I'll explain it briefly so you can look up what you want to learn more about on your own (see the list on back pages of the book). You basically need to put into your body things that will prevent, heal and calm inflammation. You also want to feed your gut bacteria all different kinds of fibre (that's a wide range of fruits and vegetables) and probiotics. The gut bacteria controls a lot of the reactions in your body, including the majority of your immune system, and if there is constant inflammation in your body due to too much sugar, alcohol, processed food or stress, there is no time and room for the natural reactions in your body to take place. If your body is under constant inflammation, it will use all its energy to heal your body instead of nourishing all the cells and enhancing happy chemical reactions. With a diet full of added hormones and artificial chemicals you are putting up roadblocks for happy intersections.

For so long I thought that sugar, white bread, pasta, and rice was bad for us solely because it made us gain weight. I didn't understand that in eating refined grains and other unnatural food sources as a part of our daily diet, our bodies and brains actually stop functioning properly. This means different things to different people; I can only say that my depression and anxiety got so much better as soon as I started to eat as natural as possible.

So don't think that eating healthy is just for people trying to look good, it is for those who want to live a happy, healthy life with all the natural happy chemicals flowing freely in their bodies. **Heal your body and mind through your gut.**

You might believe that all of your emotions are produced by and within your brain (or maybe your heart), that's what I believed for many years. I didn't think what I ate could impact how I felt emotionally. Giulia Enders shows that the gut sends signals to the brain, which stimulates areas that control our self-awareness, emotions, morality, fear, memory and motivation. Can you believe our stomach does all that!?

Our large intestine is full of a whole **universe of different bacteria** that all play a very important role in all chemical reactions happening in our mind and body. They are also in **control of our immune system** – so when we are sick or when something isn't working the way it is supposed to – the bacteria in our gut stops what they are supposed to be doing and turn their focus on healing us. When we eat all the wrong foods (like pig out on junk daily) we lose some of the "bacteria species" that can impact our whole mental state.

Different bacteria likes different fibre so that is why we need all different kinds of vegetables, (raw if possible), to get the good nutrition for the gut, immune system and brain. When our body is inflamed (we don't always feel the physical inflammations inside of our bodies) the happy chemicals such as serotonin will not be accessible for us and this can greatly affect our mood. It's so important to keep the gut bacteria happy in order to feel fantastic on all levels.

Hot Tip

I wish I knew sooner that my body is like a machine and filling it up with the wrong fuel is going to make me unhappy. Happiness is made out of chemical reactions in your body and brain and the cells of your body. The wrong fuel will prevent the happy chemicals from getting released into the body. A happy mind is run by happy fuel. I avoid everything that is made up out of artificial chemicals, because my happy chemicals and immune system will start dealing with them first, instead of making sure that my body and brain feel the best it can possibly feel.

Action:

1. Try five new vegetables each week (when you can't find any more new ones start rotating).

2. Try to eat a couple of forks full of sauerkraut every day (the gut bacteria loves everything fermented. Sauerkraut is easy and cheap to make yourself; all you need is cabbage, salt and a jar. Google has many good recipes to follow)

3. Add a probiotic supplement to your diet (probiotics are adding more of those good bacteria into your universe of helpers.)

# SECTION 6

ALCOHOL AND SHIT

This is section is about alcohol and how wrong things can get when we try too hard to fit in

IT'S ALL ONE FUCKING PARTY

My diary 16 years old
"I wake up, completely confused with doctors and Mum and Dad around me. They tell me what has happened. I almost died, couldn't breathe for myself, so they had to put me on a respirator the whole night. It was so urgent that they had to cut up all my clothes and if I hadn't had my tonsils taken out a month earlier, or just fallen asleep somewhere, I wouldn't have been able to write now. I've got three stitches in my bottom lip and drips everywhere."

"You should be so happy you are alive," the nurse said when she pulled the respiratory out of my mouth, and I returned to consciousness.

I had no idea where I was, why I was here. Bright blueish light and beeping machines surrounded me. I turned around and saw my mum and dad, sitting next to me, happy to meet my eyes, but scared of what I obviously was capable of doing to myself. As I opened my mouth to speak, I felt a pain in my bottom lip. It felt like a hedgehog was resting in the corner of my mouth. That's when they told me I had fainted at the top of some stairs at my friend's house, rolled down the staircase and split my lip in half. My friends wanted to let me sleep the booze off, but the mum in the house thought they were better off calling an ambulance (thank goodness for that). If they hadn't done that, I would have been dead. My organs had had enough and I needed a respirator to survive the night. I was sixteen years old, in the children's hospital.

"Your daughter is going to feel very bad when she wakes up," the nurse had said to my parents.

As soon as I came back to consciousness I asked what time it was; I had to go to my graduation party. I felt fine I said (I was most likely still drunk). It was June 11 and the last day of my first year of high school. My clothes had been cut up, even my golden jacket I was wearing was in pieces. Blood on my dress. My wristband said, "UNKNOWN WOMAN", how apt this description was. I wasn't able to see the tragedy in this whole situation until many years later when I actually started to care about myself. When I actually started to love myself.

The doctor wasn't happy to release me; he wanted to make sure that I didn't have a bad concussion. He said he needed to keep an eye on me over the next couple of hours. My nurse, Lina, came and moved me down to another room. I didn't need to be in emergency care anymore. Down in my new room, my mum left to get me some fresh clothes and other stuff in case we needed to spend the night. The nurse told me that they were actually celebrating the ten-year anniversary of the children's hospital wing, so there will be a few clowns and famous people coming to entertain the children. I didn't feel like a child then, but looking back at this I know that I was so much younger than I thought I was. I wish I could've felt it because then I probably would have listened to my parents and those who told me to take it easy and look after myself. But when you believe that you are older than you are, and when you don't love yourself it is hard to make clever decisions. I am just grateful now that I got a second chance because on that night, I almost lost my life.

A few Swedish celebrities came to visit me that day. I remember a hockey star, a singer and a guy from the Swedish postcode lottery. I was so excited I was running around the hospital in my white hospital dress like a mad (or drunk) person. Lisa, one of the nicest girls I have ever been friends with, came to visit me after school graduation. She let me in on all the gossip, told me who she had seen there and who had said what about who. I didn't realise at the time what a good friend she was. She didn't care about status or looking cool in front of people. She did everything with her heart, (I know it sounds corny but it's worth something). It means a lot to me that she was friends with me, because obviously, she knew the nice person in me, a person that I didn't pay almost any attention to at that time.

I had to spend the night in the hospital and my mum stayed with me. We slept on a hospital bed each, next to each other and in the morning when they asked us if we wanted breakfast I couldn't eat. I was too nauseous and shaken by the whole situation but my mum said she would love some. She had a table at the end of the bed, and she sat down to eat her dry bread with cheese, cucumber and tomatoes on, with coffee and a splash of milk from a plastic cup. It was June 12. My mum's birthday.

Hot Tip

When you are drinking you are basically altering your brain. Believing that you are going to have more fun or be more confident or whatever your reason to drink might be, is an *illusion created in your own mind. It is important to understand **why** you want to drink if you do drink, because your reason why might have something to do with not being confident enough to live out loud without having an excuse to blame it on.*

Action:

Ask yourself these questions:

1. Why do you drink? (if you answer because it tastes good then ask yourself if you would choose a non-alcoholic drink if it tasted exactly the same as the alcoholic one?)

2. Do you drink to get more confidence?

3. Do you drink to forget something for a moment?

4. Do you drink because everybody else drinks?

5. Next time you drink, ask yourself: why do I feel like I need to alter my brain right now?

Whatever your answer might be to these questions, remember that there are no right answers, you might not feel as if you need to change the way you act, or you might, that's not the point!

The point is to be able to be truthful to yourself about why you choose to act the way you choose to act! Keep asking yourself these questions from time to time and see if your answer changes – I know it has for me!

THE BOOK SHELF

My life has always needed to be extremely organised. I needed the order to feel calm because I didn't know who I was without it. I've always had the best marks in school, not because I really cared about the school subjects, but because I needed teachers to approve of me and see that I could do good even if I didn't feel good. I couldn't see my own value if I didn't perform well. I never come late to school, or any other meeting, I never skipped class to do something "better" with my time. I had to follow the rules, otherwise, I felt so lost and guilty for disappointing the people that could approve of me. I did what society wanted me to do, and I did it well, I did it by the book. The only thing my teachers could ever complain about was I was too loud in the classroom. I felt safe in school because I knew who I was there and who I was supposed to be.

If I was a bookshelf with ten shelves, one of them would be filled with boring school books in a perfect order that made sense. It would be the perfect shelf – the one I could look up to and see that as long as something is in order, it's ok. One shelf would be in absolute chaos. You wouldn't have any idea how the books ended up together. There would be rubbish in there. Razorblades. Mould. Probably some explosives. The books would be dirty, messy with missing pages and other shit that just ended up on the shelf because there was no room for it anywhere else. The rest of the shelves would be almost empty. My life was like that. Complete order, chaos and emptiness.

I've never believed that I've had a bad diet. I've always thought that I looked after myself. That's pretty ironic and absolutely untrue. I actually treated myself like absolute shit during my teenage years and early twenties. I ate everything that I thought would make me skinny. You know, short-cut shakes, shit diet choices, all processed food that said: "skinny, low-fat, sugar-free" on them and a lot of chewing gum. I ate so much chewing gum that one time when I had an earache, the throat, nose and ear doctor could see that I was chewing a lot on my left-hand side and that made my left ear ache before I even told him that's where the pain was. He could see it before I got a chance to sit down in the chair in front of him.

I can honestly say that I did everything I thought would make me skinny and look as good as all the girls around me, but I never cared or listened to how my body and mind was feeling, all that mattered was that I was skinny. I hated the way I was feeling about myself then, but I wasn't ready to take responsibility for it. I believed that the reason to why I felt bad was because my body and mind was wrong, something was missing and I had been unlucky enough to just come out the wrong way. I didn't believe that anything I did could help me feel better. That was the truth for me then, that was what I chose to see. Luckily today, that is far from what I believe, and for that I am grateful.

Hot Tip

I restricted myself, and it made me obsessed. If I could go back in time and let myself know that changing your true self never works, you will never be happy if your main goal is to change who you are and how you look. I wish I could just sit myself down, look myself in the eyes and say, "Hey you (me), instead of focusing on changing how you look, why don't we learn together how to nourish and look after our body and mind in the best way? What do you need to keep your brain happy? Because putting so much energy into trying to change who you are will only make you angrier and unsatisfied with who you are.

Action:

1. If you ever think that how you look needs to change in order for you to feel happy, try to focus on how you would like to **feel** in your own body? Write down five feelings you would love to have in your body? (e.g. confidence, power, strength, happiness, love, excitement, joy, freedom etc.)

2. How do you think you will welcome the feelings you want to feel into your life more often? Is it by punishing yourself or by cutting yourself some slack and focus on living life in a world where feelings are more important than looks? (The way you feel always shines through, so you have to focus on feeling the way you want to look!)

COCKTAIL HOUR

To contrast my restrictive and self-destructive life, I always treated myself with alcohol. A lot of it. A cold beer on a warm day, a warming drink on a cool day. If you look for it, there is always a reason to have a drink. To relax, to celebrate, to have fun, to be fun, to escape reality for a while. I've always enjoyed drinking because then, and only then, could I let go of all control and be in a place where my lack of structure and discipline was totally acceptable. If anorexia was the complete order, alcohol was my complete chaos. I didn't have to think about being perfect because I had an excuse. The reality was that I didn't need alcohol to be silly and let go of control, but my brain said that I did. That was a limitation that I created for myself, in my own head.

Illustration: Tom Falk @Artbyfalkander

Our whole lifestyle and culture in the Western World revolves around drinking. It's the norm. As young adults we were basically taught to live life for the weekend, and on the weekend you get drunk. Sundays were made for hangovers, and we were taught to hate Mondays.

It's socially accepted to vomit and piss on the streets on a Friday or Saturday night; society more or less pushed us to do it. On Monday you walked around with your friends, feeling nauseous, craving shit food, with no energy. People sort of didn't want to be around you on Mondays if you had had a relaxing weekend without any street-pissing and vomiting. If you loved life on a Monday, that was out of the norm. At least, that's how I grew up, and it took me a while to figure out that I don't have to follow those rules in society – they were only what I was open to see, not everybody's reality. It is possible to live a life where Mondays are as amazing as any other day. How? Listen to what it is that you love to do and do not compromise on that. Find a way to live with what you are passionate about and if alcohol makes you feel like shit, stop drinking it all the time!

There has never been any problem fixed through drinking. By getting shitfaced I only pushed all my problems and worries into the near future, and when I woke up from my drunken-ness, my problems, that I tried to ignore by drinking, had gotten much bigger than they were to start with.

I wish that I had of taken three months to a year off drinking in those days. That I used that time to sit down to try and get to know myself.

I wish that I could have reached out and connected to that place inside of me that truly cared about how I felt.

It would've been hard because I know that I would've felt like I was missing out on all the fun, but there would still be fun shit happening around me. I wish I had the strength then to stop drinking, to stop drinking so hard, and care about myself instead. Maybe that would have saved me a couple of years of searching because **it wasn't until I really stopped drinking for a couple of months and started to focus on what I actually wanted in life, I truly got to know myself and what I am good for.**

It wasn't until then, I felt a new calm take place in my body and I realised that **life is about passions,** not being drunk. After I had taken six months off drinking and started to focus on just letting myself live the life I want to live, I lost the need to get drunk too. I could see clearly that life doesn't have to be one way, it can be whatever way you choose to live it. **The limitations are only in our own mind.** The limitations are based on the past and with a worry for the future. **What if I told you that the past doesn't predict the future? What if I told you that anything is possible? What would you do?**

I believe that alcohol is okay. It's probably not good for anyone, but it's not just bad either. You probably hear people say you need to live a balanced life to be healthy, and maybe that sounds boring to you because the people who say that aren't getting shit faced. Balance doesn't have to be boring. It can be, if that means you "have to" put the breaks on when you crave the extreme, but balance doesn't actually mean restrictions, it's about more choices. When you are living in balance, it is sensational. I think that if sometimes you feel like getting the buzz that alcohol can give you, you have the freedom to use it to get that buzz in your life. But I used to live for that buzz, and I didn't like anything about my life without that buzz for a long time. I used the buzz to escape from my own prison but didn't realise that it only made me more trapped. That's not a balanced relationship with alcohol and that is why **I wished that I would've taken a longer break from it earlier**, or started to drink later in life, so that I would have had other fun things to do with my time, not just looking forward to the next party.

Alcohol (or smoking or drugs) are no good when it is the only thing that makes you feel connected to people. As a teenager, I used balanced drinkers to justify my excessive drinking, and that's living in a lie. That's one of many reasons I was unhappy, but also the reason why I am the well-adjusted person I choose to be today. I didn't have any tools to figure myself out. Extreme chaos and strict imprisonment were my way of balancing life, and I realise now that I was just living in two kinds of un-free realities.

Hot Tip

Since alcohol is such an accepted thing in our society, it can be hard to understand that it actually can do far more damage than good. Because it made me feel "free", I abused it. But it wasn't the alcohol that made me feel free; it was my own head. I just gave myself something to blame my feelings of freedom on.

Alcohol doesn't make you free. It makes you feel a buzz in your head, and you might say and do things that you wouldn't if you weren't drunk. But you can choose to be free anytime. Blame it on your soul. Free yourself when you are sober too, forget what people say and think about you when you are just you. It is amazing to be able to be whoever you want to be when you are truly present. Find the strength to feel what you want to feel every day. Listen to your soul, not to your brain.

Action:

1. If you drink alcohol a couple of times per month and usually feel bad the day after or don't remember everything that happened the night before; set yourself a goal to take one month off drinking (minimum). Ideally taking three months off gets the best results.

2. Make a list of ten things you like to do (without drinking)

3. Try yoga in a studio or on YouTube (Yoga with Adriene offers a free 30-day yoga challenge on her YouTube channel

4. Put your phone on airplane mode and put an alarm for 10-15 minutes. Grab a pen and a paper, put it in front of you.

   Light a candle to settle your mind and get cosy with the exercise and close your eyes. Think about who you would be and what you would do with your time if nobody influenced you to do anything. Forget all trends, all "shoulds and musts", forget how you might think that you need to behave around people, forget about group-chats, snap-chat, Instagram, Facebook. You are just you, without anything or anyone influencing you.

When the alarm goes off write down:

- Five things that make your time fly (that absorbs you).
- Five things that you would do on a weekend if your phone didn't exist (so you couldn't see what anyone else was doing).
- Five things that you would like to learn more about.

MAYA KIUSALAAS

- Five things that you have never tried but would like to try.

SECTION 7

AUTUMN TO SPRING – living on autopilot

This section deals with thoughts about hopelessness, not knowing what you want to do with your life and about feeling lost

MAYA KIUSALAAS

I REMEMBER

I stopped seeing Mia and Per way too early, but I obviously didn't know it then. I was 15 years old and wasn't actually happy enough to stop therapy, but I thought I was. I felt guilty that my parents were paying for the chaos that I allowed to define me, the mess I had created and which I sometimes thought wasn't even real. But the biggest reason to why I stopped therapy was because I was in love, and for the first time in my life, somebody loved me too.

I had been desperately in love with him for over a year before we finally got together. I used to call him from a private number and hang up when he answered, just to hear his voice. I felt so much inside, and I was so scared that nobody would ever feel like being crazy enough to do that only to hear my voice. What if nobody would feel what I felt for them? That was my biggest fear, so when we finally became a couple I couldn't risk losing him over my eating disorders and lack of self-love. I had to just be ok so I used his love to save me. I didn't know it then, I couldn't see it like that. Somebody accepted me. That somebody wasn't me, but sometimes it is hard to see the difference when you are stuck right in the middle of it with a lot of strong emotions surrounding you.

I started to eat a lot of lollies and chips just to prove that I wasn't crazy and obsessed about food and weight. As soon as I put on a bit of weight though, I panicked. The love for myself wasn't there to care for me. I just did everything I thought was normal, to look normal, but I felt anything but normal. I still drank too much when I went out. I couldn't really handle myself around alcohol, again because I didn't do anything of what I did for myself – I did it out of love for him – not to myself.

Mia, my therapist, knew that when she "let me go", but couldn't do anything about it – because you cannot help somebody who isn't aware that they need help. A few years later I was still lost. I still focused all my energy on what I wasn't, what I didn't have. I looked for misery, and I found it.

After we broke up and I didn't have him, gymnastics or anything else that made me happy and inspired in my weekly life - partying became my hobby. With partying came anxiety, a craving for shit food, tiredness, restlessness and a deep feeling of just wanting to live life from the couch. I gained and lost weight like a professional Yo-yo dietician refusing to see what I was actually doing to myself and with my life.

I worked at a kindergarten and in a school for a while after high school. One of my favourite things to do with the kids was to draw pictures of food. I remember drawing hamburgers and sausages and really feeling how that calmed my mind since I then was in a starving phase again. I was extremely anxious and depressed. Extremely lost. One lunch as I was sitting in the staff rooms massage chair I felt like I couldn't breathe. I didn't know what to do. If anyone had of asked me how I felt I would've started crying like I was one of the children at the kindergarten. I called my mum and couldn't hold it back. She told me that she would come and pick me up. I was nineteen, but I felt like I was five again when we walked home, hand in hand. She has always had my back, and my hand, my mother.

I took an evening course in writing that autumn. We did an assignment called "I remember…" and for five minutes we wrote the first thing that entered our mind after, "I remember…"

"I remember when I was a little girl and was fascinated by a world of acorns and sticks. When I could find happiness and joy in things that today are so insignificant.

I remember when my only problem was to be away from Mum and Dad.

I remember how I felt useless and nobody loved me.

I remember when people lied and said I was beautiful.

I remember when I screamed out of hatred towards myself.

I remember when I lay lonely in my bed, crying and my brother came in and told me not to spare anyone my tears; that they weren't worth it. I remember thinking that he was lying.

I remember when I laughed genuinely because I was so happy. To then realising that I wasn't.

I remember when I got scared to be happy because I realised that it wasn't forever.

I remember crying because I was angry for stuff I didn't want to be angry for.

I remember feeling that I hated you, but at the same time I hated myself because I understood that it wasn't you that I hated, it was myself. You didn't deserve that, and probably not me neither.

I remember when every night I prepared my baby bottle with milk formula and drank it every morning in bed even though I was 14."

It was a hard and dark autumn. Every morning I felt anxious until I got to work with my children in the school. When I saw them, I could shift from reverse to fifth gear in the blink of an eye. I tried to do everything to feel better but nothing I tried helped. I looked for anything to help me.

"Rosehip root, it sounds so warm. Described so warm. When the autumn winds blow cool over Stockholm with its humans walking the streets. When the sun stops visiting us as often as it has. Then, then the hope disappears. Not completely, but a little. Then the hope disappears. The hope of ever getting rid of this anxiety that is dragging me down. Not all the time, but often.

Rosehip root, it sounds so warm. Described so warm, but does it help towards the cold? The cold and the dark? The dark and the anxiety?"

One second I was so happy I almost wanted to punch people in the face so that they would understand how happy I was. The next minute I wanted to punch myself in the face for believing that I could actually be that happy. It was fireworks coming out of my chest, and I wanted to scream to the world that I love fucking everything in it. And then, with a boom, there was only a black hole left inside me, and I wondered if I could ever feel at home again. I was so scared of that black hole. And this autumn I inflated more often than ever before. I didn't know how to control it. When it was there, I just got sucked into nothingness.

But one important thing here is that I knew what happiness felt like, even if it came in short blurts. I needed to re-connect to that happiness I once knew and really try to remember what that feeling was like. I needed to remember it and visualise a life where happiness and excitement dominated my life. I needed to find faith that I could find my way back to those emotions through remembering to spend time doing what made me feel like that again. I needed to remember the happiness I once saw in the simplest thing such as an acorn!

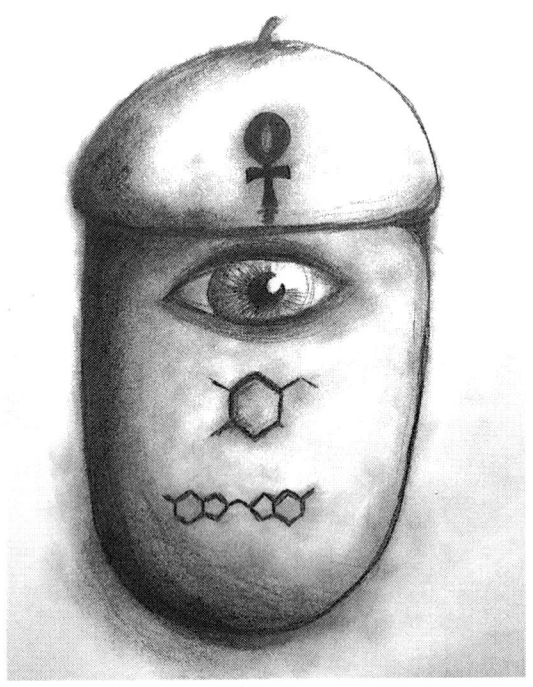

Hot Tip

If things ever feel pointless or if you feel lost, always remember those good things within you. Start small. You might take an empty page and write one good thing you hold or your life holds in the middle of the paper. For inspiration; try to connect to one thing that interest you, one person you feel excited thinking about, one good conversation you have had lately, start writing them down and then just continue to write anything that makes you feel good.

Changing your beliefs might feel like you are letting go of who you are. But actually, it's letting go of who you are not. It might seem scary to take that first step and decide that you are ready to become the best version of yourself. Yes, it might seem scary, but isn't it scarier to live in a world where those beliefs will never change? If you want to see yourself happy, then your beliefs have to change and you have to decide that you are going to be excited to be you – no matter what it takes!

Action:

1. Write down 5-10 positive beliefs that you have and/or want to have in your life. Read them every time you feel disconnected from your mind and body

2. Really feel that what you read is true and possible (because it is)

e.g. I believe that I am good enough the way I am

I believe that my body is worthy of being looked after.
I believe that I am worthy of feeling loved, being loved and loving myself.
I believe that I can be whoever I (fucking) want to be in this world.
I believe that as long as I nurture my body and soul with nutrition and love, let it express itself through its real emotions, and I respect it; I will feel content with who I am.
I trust my body and my soul.
I believe that I can do anything I want, I only have to truly believe that I can.
I believe that I am limitless.

Now it's your turn!

SHOOT ME

My diary- 20 years old
It was in the middle of the night, and Mum found me in the kitchen with a knife and a chopping board.

"But my little darling, what are you doing?"

"Nobody loves me anyway. Mum, do you know how I feel? You know what I wish for? I just want somebody to shoot me here and here and here so that I end up in a coma and then wake up. They might understand that they miss me then."

Mum took me to emergency psychiatric care. I couldn't speak. I felt fake for being there. I didn't want to die; I just wanted to be happy. I shouldn't be there. Mum sat down with the doctor and tried to justify why I should get help. "She doesn't love herself, she starves, vomits, hurts herself. She needs to love herself, and I don't know how to make her see that she is the most amazing girl." I couldn't breathe because that was it. I didn't love myself.

I felt so small, so insignificant. Whatever 'me' was, I certainly didn't know her.

I have had enough. No one should have to feel like this. No strength. Only darkness. No peace. Crying out of loneliness.

Abandonment. So horrible, gone and lost. No. Fuck that! I need help. Help to feel good. – 20 years old.

Lost. That's what I felt. I felt as if I owed to my friends and family to do what they wanted me to do, like spend time going out partying with my friends, to not be boring and then not look too anxious and sad in front of my parents, because they had put up with me and my sadness for so long. I owed them to be happy and excited to live my life, but I wasn't. I felt like the world was out there and I was standing somewhere just frozen, not knowing where I should or wanted to go. Lost. I felt as if there was no purpose with anything. I knew that there should be a purpose, only I had no idea how to figure out what purpose meant to me. I felt a pressure, as if I had to know who I wanted to be in this world, what I wanted to do, but I had no fucking clue. Lost. I felt like life was so overwhelming, there are so many things everyone "should" be doing, but I didn't understand why. Lost.

There is a spiral here where at some point I got so absorbed in what was wrong in the moment that I started to live in that wrong moment forever – because it was all I focused on, it was all I saw and thought about. In this world there are different types of prisons; some that we get sent to because we have broken the law and some that we put ourselves in without even knowing. The prison is a life on autopilot. This gets even clearer after you finish school and have to create some kind of rhythm in your own life. Routines are safe and stable, they are like traffic lights that protect us from oncoming cars and make it easier for us to interact with other drivers - but in themselves, the traffic lights are worth nothing. We have commonly agreed to trust them, but they don't help us with reading our maps. They don't show us the right direction – their job is only to keep us safe. Routines are similar to traffic lights in the way they keep us safe on the road – but we all know how annoying they are when traffic backs up and interrupts the flow of driving. Routines can be like that. They can stop us from the flow of life – so it's important to question your routine, especially if you want to live in the flow of life and go wherever life wants to take you.

Hot Tip

Not knowing what to do with yourself and your life is a nagging feeling. I used to feel flat out scared because I didn't have any idea on my direction. Feeling like I was never good enough didn't help, it just meant that I didn't believe that I could ever be a valuable contributor to any job or to myself. What I know now is this: Life is about being happy, full of love and excited for whatever comes your way. Life isn't meant to be controlled; it's meant to be lived.

I had controlled my life with an iron fist for so long, then suddenly, I understood that I was missing out on the flow of life when I did so. I now constantly ask myself what I love to do that makes time fly. If anything new pops up, I embrace it and introduce it to my life. I no longer try to be in charge of every situation, I listen to what life is offering and then take the most from it.

Understand that what you love to do and what makes you excited is exactly what you are supposed to do. Don't fight with yourself over what you 'should do' or 'must do', help yourself live a life where you can have fun all the time. When you realise what you desire to do, don't ever compare it to what other people are doing. We are all unique, remember? And that makes for a big world where everything is possible. Many people do things they aren't passionate about for status or safety, money or because they were stuck on autopilot and didn't even stop to ask, "Will this make me happy?"

Is it worth it? All those cold sweating nights from stress, all that time wasted in life? My rule is to never compare passions with others but to be inspired by those who follow what they love doing.

Action:

1. Next time you are bored; explore your hobbies, or better, find new ones. Today you can learn just about anything from YouTube or the Internet. Maybe you want to learn how to cook or ferment your own food, do yoga, paint, draw, run, do makeup, sing, stretch, learn a new language, build robots or learn the whole dance to Beyoncé's "Single Ladies". Almost everything you can think of has a tutorial. Get creative with it, and do things that make you happy! (You might even call a friend or a family member you would like to get closer to and invite him/her over to learn something new with you?)

2. What is the flow of life? What does it mean to you? How are you interacting with life's own

flow; are you riding on it or trying to control it? Explain to yourself or a friend how you are either in or outside the flow though coming up with one example when you tried to control what happened to you in life and another where you worked with what life had to offer.

e.g. To me, the flow of life means everything that happens that is out of my own control. It is everything that is offered to me, all people I meet, every conversation that happens (or doesn't happen), it is all the possibilities and all the pathways I have in front of me. When I am in the flow I am connected to my inner self and I follow what makes me feel good. I don't do things just because I "should" do them; I know why I do what I do. I know I study things that I am interested in or read books I love because it absorbs me. Sometimes I might not love what I am doing in the moment but I know that I will be grateful that I did what I did in the future – I try to view it as if I'm saving my future self from having to do it then.
Your turn!

MY CONCRETE MUM

Mum has always wanted me on her lap, always kissed me and hugged me. Not a day has gone passed without my parents telling my brothers and I how much they love us. My lack of self-love must have come from somewhere else. Somewhere deeper rooted than that.

My mum is a perfect example of a person who decided to finally follow her passions. She has been feeling lost since forever, always working with people in need of care. She is an amazing carer who never just sits out her time; she puts her soul into making the best time for the people she is looking after. When it comes to caring and taking care of people, especially those who aren't in a position to speak for themselves, she always do the absolute best for the person she is looking after, no matter who gets in her way; she speaks her truth for the sake of the people who need her, no questions asked. She never tries to sweet-talk the bosses or lick their butts. She has spent a lot of time helping others, but in her own life, she has been feeling lost and hasn't been helping herself out. Something has been missing for her to feel fulfilled.

Concrete has always been fascinating to her. For a decade there was a big bag of concrete mix up in our attic collecting dust. It is the timelessness of concrete that gives her goose bumps. The fact that you can create anything with it, and the possibility to create all different types of concrete makes her imagination expand to eternity. For ten years she believed that she had to take care of people because society accepts that kind of job, and that would give her money to pay rent. And even though she did an amazing job doing so, it didn't make her time fly. It wasn't what she was passionate about. She lived her life following the rules, but she wasn't happy doing so.

Suddenly she realised that she had to spend time doing what really made her happy and stop focusing on what she thought she "should" be doing. She had spent all of this time looking after people whilst her fingers were just itching to play with concrete. She signed up for a night course in concrete art and learnt how to make the most out of the material. Today she is speaking the tongue of concrete, and she makes the most magnificent creations. It is raw and rough, just like herself. She makes tables, bird baths, big tubs, small plates, door knobs, fountains, candleholders and everything that comes through love. Once she realised that following the rules of society and playing to that collective acceptance wasn't what made life complete, she finally became happy, proud and excited with how she spends her time

Look at her website www.inkabetong.se and see for yourself.

If you take away one thing from this book let it be this:
Don't ever think that you cannot do what you are passionate about doing. Do whatever you do with love, and if you don't love it – don't do it, unless you do it for a purpose that you love.

(Cleaning a baby's butt is an example – you don't love dealing with poo, but you love for the baby to feel amazing). Do what makes your time fly, and make a plan on how you can live based on that. Don't let your inner critic convince you that you are not good enough to do what you love to do, ever!

Hot Tip
There are so many things I wished that I would have done back when I was a teenager, but I kept on telling myself that I

wasn't good enough and that it was too late to start learning something new (IT'S NEVER TOO LATE, and no matter how old you feel when you are a teenager, I promise you that you will look back at yourself and wish that you understood that you actually weren't that "old".) Take advantage of life, every day.

Action:

1. Write down three things that you secretly dream about doing but think that it is too late to start. It might be horse riding, netball, singing, swimming, gymnastics, soccer, tennis, producing music, making videos, making apps, anything.

2. Do your research and see if there are any local places where you can try some of them out, go to the library and borrow a book about the subject, research and see if there are any free podcasts about your new hobby, or ask your old friend YouTube/internet for advice.

SECTION 8

ORDER AND CHAOS

This section is about frustration and about feeling like your whole world is spinning around you so you have to find things to hold on to and learn to control your mind in order to stay alive.

PLEASE FIX ME

"I will figure this out." I told myself staring at the fucking mathematics book and some stupid equation I just simply couldn't solve in my brain. "I can't do this." I thought. Except I needed to understand it because I identified myself as the perfect student. I followed orders in school, I had to have the best marks. Doing as I was told in school protected me from my inner chaos of not knowing who I was. If I can follow the rules, I felt peace because, at least there, I was someone. I wasn't lost. But math was, and still is, too logical for me. Give me something abstract, something existential, and I'll be able to talk forever about it. Can't there just be a grey zone in math?

My dad tried to help me understand and although I should be grateful for his effort, I felt this electrical irritation and frustration bubble up from the darkness of my soul. Can't I just not get it? Why do I have to get it? I don't fucking get it!

Not long after that I tore one of the pages out of my book and ate it before I threw the rest out the window. (Yes, that actually happened).

I've always put pressure on myself to be the best at everything. And if I couldn't be the best I "wanted" to be the worst at it. I have never liked to be mediocre. It's everything or nothing in the most literal sense imaginable. This is a reoccurring pattern in my life. I had to be the best in all school subjects, the best at gymnastics and most of the time I didn't actually care (my soul didn't care), but I felt like other people cared (my brain told me that and I chose to believe it) so I fought to get approval. Most spiritual people would probably say that it was my ego I was trying to satisfy. The thing with the brain and the inner critics inside is that when you start trying to love your life by pleasing the inner critics, you will enter a rabbit hole with no ending. The inner critics will always try to find new things that you need prove yourself in. They never get satisfied and always make you see the faults in every situation. The ego wants you to lose your gratitude and when you forget how to be grateful you also lose your ability to enjoy the present moment. What I learned is you might as well stop trying to please the ego and the inner critics and focus on pleasing your soul instead.

One way of getting out of that rabbit hole is to practice gratitude for what you have now and what you appreciate about your own efforts. It's when you lose the ability to enjoy the moment that life gets pretty dark – practising gratitude in the moment is like being given a little torch to see in the dark. When frustration comes and you feel like you have to do something a certain way or else… What is that, "or else?" I tell you what it is; it is nothing. It is a made up emotion that nobody but you is worried about, so you might as well stop worrying about it too!

There is never just one right way of doing things, remember that! If you really want something in the future; like a job you haven't got the grades for or an education you haven't got the money for or whatever it may be; there are hundreds of different ways to achieve what you want to achieve. If it doesn't happen now, it will happen in the future, if you decide to make it happen and are willing to do whatever it takes.

The pressure I put on myself made me crazy. I needed to escape. The reality is that nobody expected anything from me but my ego. My extreme personality grasped for things to control, things to be the best at, just so that people would approve of me. I needed rules, routines, safety and order in my life so that I wouldn't drown in my emotional chaos. I think that is one of the reasons why I developed anorexia and got obsessed with being sick, skinny and good in school, because it gave me control and excuses for why I couldn't achieve things. What it didn't give me was life, excitement, confidence, happiness, love and freedom. I was so afraid of failing that I couldn't live – I could only survive the day.

If only I knew that it was up to me to change that. It was always up to me to reach inside and find the power to say, "fuck you" to all of those made up expectations, all that fear, and dive into the flow of life. The truth is that we choose in every moment who we want to be, and every second is a chance for us to start over. Don't wait to get ready, because you might end up waiting for ten years like I did. Jump into the flow now, you'll be okay, better than okay, you'll be alive.

Someone said something (pardon my inability to supply you with a source) along the lines of, "enlightenment is to find the power to walk through a door, overcome an obstacle, and look back to realise that it was never a door or an obstacle, it was just in your own mind". That is how I felt when I started to live my own life without constantly trying to please all the self-made expectations. There was never an expectation, it was just in my head.

In my school many people sort of knew their "place" and they accept it because they believe that's what was expected of them. The truth is that it's not real. If you choose to you can come to school and behave in the exact same way that you behave at home with your parents or with your grandparents.

Notice the difference in how you speak about yourself and others depending on who you're talking to. You might say, like I said, that teachers expect you to get good marks and your friends expect you to be fun, crazy or reckless all the time, but what would happen if you went against it? That might not mean that you change who we are and how you act, (unless what you do makes you sad or unconfident), simply be aware of the fact that we do change the way we speak and behave depending on who we surround ourselves with. It's a great awareness to have.

Hot Tip

Pretend for a second that you don't know anything about anything. You don't know any fashion "rules", you don't know what is popular and trendy at the moment, you don't know what topics people like to talk about, nothing. Pretend that there is nothing that you need to do to be "someone", there is no "cool people" and no "uncool" people. There are just people, same as you.

This exercise is similar to an earlier one, but with what you just read might bring up some different answers.

Action:

1. Write down three things that you believe that "people" expect of you?

   Ask yourself:

    a) Do they really have those expectations or is it just in your own mind?
    b) What would happen if you chose not to meet those expectations?
    c) What would you do with your time if you didn't worry about living up to those expectations?

2. If nobody cared about what you were doing, what would you like to do? Think about how what you want to do would make you feel?

e.g. I would love to sing and dance because it makes me feel full of life. I would love to write because when I write I feel connected to my emotions. I want to ride horses because it makes me feel free. I want to create and design my own clothes because I feel like that is an expression of myself.

3. If you never had to work for money, what would you do with your time? Every day, take

one step closer to that life through dreaming, planning, learning, reading about it.

MAYA KIUSALAAS

CREATING SPACE

As people in society, we seem to have a soft spot for negativity. I have to stop myself sometimes from not spreading gossip about who is in what sticky situation and instead focus on sharing as many positive stories as possible.

Fear and doom are played to us on the news, in advertising, gossip magazines and in the conversations we have every day. I get caught up in it too if I'm not paying attention. What I've learned now is that **when I stop focusing on my fear or anxiety and start to explore a world where positivity is the norm, I see more positivity and feel more positive.**

I deleted all my news apps with notifications from my phone and turned off my TV-news-background-noise. I used to be worried that I would miss out on big news or not be in the loop with what is going on in the world, but we are living in a world where news stories are overflowing our channels, it is almost impossible not to be updated. Even if I don't read the news myself I always hear what is going on through the people I interact with and I feel as if I value my conversations with people more.

A part of me (most likely my ego) wanted to know things before people told me. I liked being the one "breaking the news". Today I love when people share with me things that I don't know yet. I have learnt that it is only when I listen to others that I am able to learn something new from them.

I started to meditate for 15 minutes every day (I used a meditation app called *One Giant Mind* in the beginning) and I created space for good thoughts in my mind. Before that I used to mainly talk to people about negative stuff we had in common, maybe about people who lived differently to the way I was living then, and I used to bring attention to what was going wrong in my life, sharing only negative experiences and emotions I was dealing with as an effort to lighten up or start a conversation. For some reason it was easy to connect with people through things we have in common that we don't like, partly I think that this is because we are afraid to come off as bragging, but also partly because it is more revealing, sharing a story with someone that had gotten you moved, touched or made you feel really happy. "What if they don't feel what I feel?" I used to think. Soon I realised that if I spent time only thinking and talking about depression, anxiety and things I didn't like, my mind had no room for happiness. In fact, because I spent all my time thinking and talking about shit I had no time left to focus on happiness, health and love.

I started using my time thinking about a happy life, a happy dream and everything good around me. I noticed that my mood lifted.

I used to write little stories where I pictured myself walking down the streets of Stockholm or Melbourne with a feeling of being complete. I smile at people I meet in my stories, say, 'hi' and almost dance along because I am so happy. I walk past a bookshop and I see one of my books in the window and I almost can't believe it. I see my partner, Adrian coming along towards me, smiling and we would go off into the rest of the world and just go wherever we feel happy going. I would keep these stories with me on the days where living felt a little harder and as soon as I felt that piece of paper in my pocket I would remember to try to feel like I am that girl in the story right now.

If I want to have freedom and positivity, I have to create space in my brain for that to appear.

There is no way that's going to happen if I kept thinking about and being afraid of the opposite.

Life is about finding a way out of struggles; it's about learning and constantly growing. The struggles and obstacles I've overcome have been many, and they are unique, so are yours.

I know never to compare my journey to another person's. If I did compare, I would sound like the biggest wimp. Compared to some people, who have been through trauma, abuse and savage pain, I've had a seemingly easy life. That's the thing though; the happiest of people can be found in a place with the shittiest conditions, and the most haunted souls can live life in the most amazing communities. That just proves how what we think about is what we live.

What makes us who we are, how we experience reality, has to do with what's going on inside of us. Connections to our emotions are probably the only thing that can set us free in this world; because it isn't until we know how we feel, here and now, that we can change and work towards feeling how we would love to feel tomorrow.

I was so connected to my anxiety and my depression and my guilt that when happiness and excitement came and visited I felt as if I became a firework with happiness, joy, lust, expression, energy and excitement exploding out of my head and I just wanted to do everything at the same time. I also knew that any second it would disappear, the show would be over soon and I hated that. At first, I hated the fact that I didn't know how to make the good feelings last, but later I understood that emotions coming and going also means that the anxiety too would disappear. Instead of being scared of it coming, I started to look forward to when it left, this is a good way of flipping a perspective. I looked and waited for happiness and freedom instead and life suddenly got a little bit more exciting.

We all naturally strive for balance but then and there, my balance was anything but natural. I lived with my feet in two worlds. In one world I was a person who completely followed the rules, an excellent student, and from that world I then dove deep into a chaotic reality where I was drinking and starving myself.

What happened when I stopped accepting drinking as my only outlet was that I felt less shit and had more time living in a place where I had energy to explore emotions that made me feel good. Re-learning what it felt like to feel good made me curious of what other things I could change in my life in order to feel even better. Soon I started to pay attention to nutrition and I learnt more about what my body actually needed to feel physically good (not just to "look good"). I slowly got rid of artificial chemicals and hormone pumped food and started to live more naturally. The more I started to play around with a lifestyle that made me feel good a new type of balance started to take up space in my life. The more I actually started to naturally look after myself, the less anxious and chaotic I felt. I started to experience a natural balance in my life where I didn't have to compare myself with others. I knew that I made good choices because I listened to what my body and mind truly desired.

Hot Tip

My partner and absolute best friend, Adrian, taught me something really good about addictions, habits and balance. Back then I only had two extreme gears; I was either the perfect student or a chaotic party girl. Neither of my two versions nourished my soul or gave me a true purpose in life (with true purpose I mean something that kept my brain curious, made me curious of learning and get better at something, contributed to happiness to my life).

I used one part of me to please others and the other part to make it excusable not to please others. What Adrian taught me was to never let my extremes take over, because to take over means that it leaves no room for anything else. The secret he taught me was to have many healthy obsessions and let them balance each other. I got really interested in health (real health, not nutrition for looks), I started to listen to podcasts that interested me and taught me new things, read books that interested me, dedicate more time to writing, exercise to feel good and rest to complement the exercise.

When I did that I didn't have that much time to "only" be perfect and chaotic. I had to balance my time between learning about health, practicing my writing, being with my friends and family, running, yoga and relaxing. If I focus too much on exercise I won't be happy, but if I only relax I won't feel good either.

Relaxing is amazing if you do it consciously and it is the same with so many other things too. If I only live a life where being perfect in school matters and I spend all my time studying

I will not have time doing anything else, like being with my friends and family.

Action:

1. Write down everything that you give attention to during the week. Is there one or two things on your list that take so much attention and time from you that it overrules other things?

e.g. If I am obsessed with working out and I never let my body rest I might get so tired I will miss out on hanging out with my friends or finishing my homework. Or if I am too absorbed with going out late and living life in chaos I will not have time or energy to look after my health or pay attention to my hobby.

2. See if what do in a regular week is balanced. If there is not that much on the list, say you are only dedicating your time to two things like I was; Write down five things that you could start implementing into your weekly routine. (Stuff you like)

e.g. Start going for one long walk per week, cook dinner one night per week because I would love to learn more about nutrition and taste, read books that allow me to expand my imagination, write songs and learn an instrument to express my deepest thoughts through or paint through my emotions.

MEDITATION

I never used to believe that I could find peace meditating. To me, just the thought of sitting still, listening to my own breathing for 15 minutes sounded like a complete nightmare. Just the thought of sitting down and do nothing made my hands itch. I felt like there was nothing I could possibly do in this world that would be more stressful than meditation. That was before I knew what meditating meant. No one had described it in a way that spoke to me.

As I started to actually link the pieces of the puzzle together, one by one, I realised that where I put my focus controlled my whole world – that I am what do and feel. What I think about controls my emotions and my emotions control my thoughts. When I woke up back in the day the first thing I thought about was how my body looked; I forced myself to do sit ups and push ups just to feel that I had started to burn fat from the get-go. I looked in the mirror for what I wanted to improve without seeing the parts of me that I liked. It was as if those parts weren't worth any attention – only the "shit" parts. I had trained my brain to see what needed to be changed – now I needed to re-train it!

It felt fake to me in the beginning when I started to actively pay attention to what I liked about myself. It was hard work, looking in the mirror and stopping myself from listening to the voices that talk shit about me. I had to give space for that voice that talked about the good stuff, it was a challenge. At the start, I never thought that I would be able to believe the nice voice but the more I listened to it the more I understood that I am actually a nice, kind-hearted and fun person to be around, if I allow myself to be.

It's like a closed circle, like an emotional ecosystem. We all know what happens to our muscles if we train them and give them the right nutrition and building blocks; they grow. Our brain is a muscle, a very important one. With a little bit of practice we can exercise, train and grow those muscles. Meditation is a way of working out the focus muscles in our brain. If we learn to focus on what makes us thrive we are able to connect to what truly makes us happy. Then it's up to us to go out, say, "fuck you," to expectations and unwritten rules when necessary and get good shit to happen.

When I felt overwhelmed, like I had no control over what was happening in life, when just living felt hard and like, too big of a project, I was taught to be mindful and focus on what I could see, smell, feel and experience in the moment. What have I got here and now that I can do?

With meditation and mindfulness, I was able to change focus from the critical voices in my head to actual things that were true in the moment, like how good my dad's cooking smelt and how the light from outside created a reflection of the room in the TV. The more I started to pay attention to what I had in the moment I saw more possibilities to what I could do with my time. With meditation, I learnt that it is possible to take a step back and just observe the destructive thoughts that emerged in my brain and I realised that I could distance myself from them. Sometimes they told me that I looked wrong in everything, that all my friends looked better than me, that everybody just pretended that they liked me but they really just felt sorry for me, that people thought that I was lazy and never helped, my clothes weren't right, my body wasn't right. That's what they said and that's what I believed was true until I learnt that those voices are just thoughts – nothing real! They didn't have power over me. I realised that just because they are thoughts and voices in my head they are not what and who I am. I am the power behind the thoughts that can choose if I want to listen to the critics or focus on the positive, motivated and curious thoughts instead.

The more I meditated and practiced distancing myself from the negative forces in my mind, the less effective they were. Finally, I didn't have to dive into chaos and control. The extremes naturally levelled out.

There are heaps of meditation apps and YouTube channels out there that can teach you different technics of meditation. There is no right or wrong way of training your focus. I love to incorporate breathing in my meditation simply because I feel like I clear my whole system through deep breathing. I can focus on my breath, observe my thoughts and oxidise my whole body at the same time. Sometimes I do it on the bus or train, sometimes I sit like a monk with lit candles. Sometimes I just walk somewhere and choose to use it as a meditative walk where I connect to my breathing and focus on nothing but what is going on in the exact moment.

Hot Tip

Don't be scared of losing contact with your anxiety and depression: they are not who you are (unless you choose them to *be). If you are feeling anxious, depressed or sad; it is, like Kelly Brogan says so beautifully, **your body's way of signalling to you that something inside of you needs attention.** In the same way, you get a cough or a sore throat when you have a virus, **anxiety is your body's way of communicating to you that something is up.** Listen to what it is trying to say!*

Action:

1. Write down three emotions that take up most time of your life.

   Think about where in your body they are located. Do they make you feel good or bad? What situations, events, words or actions usually trigger each emotion?

   Think about how long you have had these feelings for. Write down anything else you notice about these emotions. If you cannot find words for them, express them through a drawing, what is the shape, the colour, the size or the texture?

2. You are not alone, even if you might think you are. However hard it might seem or feel,

telling someone how you feel always releases some of the pressure. Find an adult that you can talk to about your feelings. Anyone that you trust, your parents, brother, sister, family friend, your friends parents, your uncle, aunt, grandparent, school counsellor, a teacher, a cousin, priest, neighbour, sports coach, your hairdresser, a doctor, your pet (they are great listeners but they may not be able to offer the concrete advice you might need). If you don't know what to say, maybe start with asking them "have you ever felt like…?"

3. Download a meditation app (try using Headspace or One Giant Mind), choose a YouTube channel or set your timer for 10-15 minutes. Do this every day for a month.

One day you might just connect for five minutes, one day you might sit for 30. Every minute is valuable!

If you don't like the first few meditations you try, keep looking. There are so many, you will find one that works for you, or try a change in location. You might find you connect better outside, in the garden or park or at the beach. Remember, you are unique so find that path that works for you.

Candle flames make great focus points so try gazing into a flame and let your thoughts soften. If you notice those critics or anxieties pop up your mind when you meditate, that's okay, acknowledge that they are there and let them go. That might mean you ask them to leave now, or you thank them for showing up, it might mean you think of an opposite thing after each one or imagine them flying away and out of you. A great way to get started is to think only about breathing and every part of the breath as it goes all the way through you, into your body, your lungs and then around your whole body and out again.

SECTION 9

BACK THEN

This section deals with lack of motivation, depression and the how to feel comfortable in anyone's company or situation.

MY WORLD IS A COUCH

Back then, when depression consumed me and I didn't know how to care for myself, a wasted Sunday or Monday meant nothing. I could live through the TV instead of living my own life. I used alcohol to numb my brain. To stop thinking. To breathe. I justified my way of living with being completely hung over. The best thing ever was when MTV showed a "The Hills" or a "Geordie Shore" marathon on a head pounding Sunday. I could just lie on the couch eating, sleeping and watching the fighting, partying and backstabbing that took place on the reality shows.

I loved anything that distracted me from my own life. I loved sleeping because I didn't have to think, I didn't have to deal with people's expectations, and I didn't have to deal with my own expectations or thoughts

Mum walked past me as I was 'slothing' on the couch, last night's makeup smeared around my eyes. She looked at me with pain in her eyes and told me to go out for a walk. "How are you?" she asked with a worrying tone that made me feel more stressed than comforted. Her eyes begged me to just live my life, not waste it on the couch in front of MTV. But I couldn't, I fucking loved MTV. I don't know what I would've done without it at that time. I was stuck in a reality where to party was to live, and the weekdays were just a waiting game for the next event.

Mum put up a mirror at knee-height so I could see myself laying in my corner of the couch. My holy couch corner where I was protected from the real world, from the real people. Where I was protected from myself. She never admitted that putting that mirror there was an attempt to make me see what I was doing to myself, but I am sure it was, if only on her own subconscious level. The mirror in itself didn't change anything, but looking back it really did reflect what I allowed my life to be like. What I settled with. That corner was my favourite place in the world then, and if that doesn't say a lot about how little I valued life and myself, I don't know what does.

My parents wanted to give my brothers and I the freedom of being children for as long as possible. They didn't give us any adult responsibilities because they both had to grow up way too early when they were kids. They loved for us to just focus on what made us happy. They wanted us to be outdoors, playing with friends, practising music and art. You could say that my only responsibility in life was to be happy, and deep down I felt like such a failure when I couldn't be happy. My parents had given me one responsibility in life and I couldn't get it right.

Hot Tip

I wish I could teach my younger self to explore her core values: to put her focus on the things that she truly valued in life: love, fun and self-expression. Instead of that she focused on status and climbing some imaginary social ladder which was never going to fulfil her desire for a fun, healthy and a rewarding place to be present in. Competing can sometimes put your focus on other people's values, which is not a road that leads to feeling more content, unless you compete in something you are passionate about. Let your focus be on what you value most.

It is always good to think about what you want in your life, even if those things might change through your life. The more you know what you want and take action to learn about what makes you happy the less lost you feel. The older you get, the more you will be able to choose what you want to do with your life based on what you value the most! If you constantly do things that you don't value too highly just because you think that it is what you "should" be doing, chances are that you won't feel as free and excited, as you want to. As you need to.

Action:

1. Write down 5 to 10 things that you want in your life

e.g. Happiness, love, friends, family, a fun job, animals, excitement, positivity, optimism, freedom, money, health, wellness, opportunity, possibility, honesty, structure, routines, patience, harmony, nature, creativity

2. Ask yourself **why** these things mean a lot to you?

   "Why am I doing what I am doing?" Is a question that you can never ask yourself too many times!

3. Whenever you choose to do or not do something/say something, ask yourself, why am I doing/not doing this? What do I achieve if I do or if I do not?

e.g. Why am I wearing this makeup/shoes/dress/bag? Is it because I think that other people will think something of me when I wear this or because I really love how I feel right now?

My turn: Why am I writing this book?

I am writing this book because if I can help anyone out there who is experiencing some, or all of the feelings I used to experience and open their minds up to the freedom I now feel, it means that I have done something good. My life has a purpose! And I love to see as many people as possible excited to live their life with purpose! Plus, I learn so much about myself by writing all of this, which is an amazing by-product.

Now it's your turn!

PIECE OF SHIT

When I dig for dirt in my past, I realise how selfish I've been to my whole family. I knew it then, I know I was hurting them through not caring for myself, but I didn't know how to deal with what I was feeling. Not even for them. My brother was dating one of my good friends, and I'm pretty sure that I destroyed their relationship simply by being selfish and needy. I wanted his full attention. I didn't want to share.

I have always looked at my older brothers and seen that they had the potential to be anything they ever wanted to be. To me, they are both geniuses. I depended on them making it in this world so that they could support me. I never played with the idea that I could make it on my own, whatever that means. I think that I saw in them everything I didn't see in myself. So when my youngest older brother wanted to hang out with my friend, I couldn't stand it. I was 17 years old and I could feel that it was so selfish of me, and I did hate myself for screaming at him to come home alone and leave her out, but I didn't know how to shut my own ego out and allow him, them, to be happy together.

I hated that part of me, but I didn't know how to distance myself from it. I loved her, I loved him, but I couldn't stand them being together because my ego was set that I needed him way more than she did. (This is something I have learnt to understand now, but I couldn't handle it then). In my head, I lived in a tragedy and I couldn't let other people live a normal, happy life around me. I was jealous, but couldn't see it. I forced them to put me and my "happiness" first. It was quite a crazy and sad situation that I truly wish I could re-live and do differently. If I could I would've allowed my brother to live his life, with his emotions and not drag him down with me. Imagine if I would've looked at their love and what they had and allowed myself to dream about experiencing that for myself again instead of letting my jealousy take away the good feelings that they both had.

When the same brother broke his leg, I got madly jealous. I was 13-years old when I wrote in my diary *"well, well, fucking well, of course Saci has broken his stupid leg and gets all the attention. Nobody cares about me"*.

When other people got attention for being hurt my jealousy awoke too. It really made me feel frustrated to see how people could understand the pain he was in. I had no idea how to show or speak about the pain

I was in because it didn't hurt like a broken leg, it hurt without any pain, inside. It was a feeling of just not being worth anything mixed with a frustration of trying to figure out what to do to feel worth something.

I couldn't bear my brother being injured and looked after. Not because I didn't feel for him; because I wanted to be the one that was injured, I felt so alone when other people needed help more than myself.

When I went to clinics and doctors for treatment I had to fill in all these forms and they asked me if I ever felt pleasure in killing insects or other tiny animals. I don't get pleasure in hurting other things but I got a lot of pleasure out of hurting myself. I didn't get pleasure out of flaunting the injuries

though, because I knew they weren't real. I felt like a fraud. I had made them up, just like I had made up who I was.

Before I was old enough to realise what I was doing, I used to hide from my parents and family just to see how long it would take them to notice that I was gone. I remember laying behind the desk in my room feeling so frustrated because no one was looking for me. When I finally could hear their voices wondering where I was, I felt this wave of calm in my whole body. But I didn't let them know where I was. I let them get worried because that made me feel good. I wish that I could've understood that I didn't have to hide, be hurt or sad for my parents and friends to love me. Just me being me is more than enough.

Hot Tip

I wish I could reach out a hand and ask myself to enjoy life, stop worrying, and spend time with people who make me feel worthy and happy. I would tell myself to spend time with people that I don't have to prove myself to, or better yet, understand that I don't have to prove myself to anyone.

You know when you have it made when you can just observe how others are, not judge them or compare yourself, just do what sits and feels good within. I wish that I could have been friends with everyone without thinking that I had to prove anything or do anything different. Most of all I wish I could understand that I didn't have to prove anything to myself. I am good enough just the way I am. If I truly understand that, then what other people do actually wouldn't affect me.

We can create stories in our head that have nothing or little to do with truth or reality. We might even choose to believe that made up mess over the facts that we have in front of us. Our ego wants answers. This is where we need to learn to separate fact from story.

Do you ever get lost in what's in your own head instead of looking at facts and the bigger picture? If someone you know doesn't smile and say, 'Hi' when they pass you do you make it all about you and let your head go crazy with some made up story?
"They must hate me"
"Someone has told them something bad about me."
"I'm not interesting." Or
"God, She is a such a bitch to me!"

What if it's not about you at all? Maybe they were thinking about something and didn't even see you there. Maybe they were waiting for you to say Hi first because they feel insecure and lack confidence, maybe they are having a really rotten day and just can't manage a smile right now. It's so easy to think inside our own heads and believe the world revolves around us, the truth though is other people have their own shit going on. You will never have the power to read a person's mind. No matter how well you know them and love them. The only way to know what they are thinking is to ask them.

Action:

1. Think about a time or a situation where something happened (you didn't get invited to somewhere, you got a cryptic text, did or didn't get a hello from someone) and you made up your own story about why it happened without having any other facts besides the fact that it happened.

    a) What actually happened? (What is the only true fact/facts you have?)
    b) What story did you create around it?

    Instead of making up a story based on insecurity and fear, next time, go straight to the source and ask them about it instead. It will save you a lot of unnecessary pain, anxiety and wonders.

2. Communicate with your family or the people you live with. If you have had a conflict, wait until you feel calm inside and the heat of the moment has left.

Tell them as a group or individually, that sometimes you feel like _____ (fill in the blanks) and that might cause you to act out in anger or sadness but it doesn't have anything to do with them. Ask them to try and understand you and not get angry with you. If you need space when you feel emotional, ask them to give you space. If you feel like you just want a hug and for them to tell you ten things that they love about you – ask for that!

MAYA KIUSALAAS

WHAT AM I DOING WITH MY LIFE?

Once again the morning arrives, sings my alarm tone, 6.20am, as usual. I roll out of bed onto the cold floor. Sit-ups and push-ups in the dark. It smells like fried onion from the kitchen. Dad has made his usual omelette and is doing today's crossword. I start making some coffee at the same time as I put three eggs in the frying pan. Two for mum and one for me. I love preparing her breakfast. She is in some form of parallel universe when she wakes up. It can take her up to an hour to prepare her breakfast if I'm not there, and for me, it seems automatic, so I might as well. When she comes back to our universe, her breakfast is served, and there we are. Some mornings my anxiety is so heavy I can't even look at my mum. I stare out in the nothingness. Mum usually asks questions that make me lose my appetite. She might ask when I finish work today, and the omelette turns sour. Some mornings are lighter than others. But no matter how I feel I need that coffee routine with her in the mornings. I am 19 and our coffee time makes me feel safe, even when we don't talk to each other.

As I pulled out the chair in our living room, I felt this frustration of not knowing where the fuck I'm going in my life. I compared myself to all people who were interested in something, who knew that they were good at something. I had nothing I was good at, except socialising I suppose (and to be honest I wasn't even too good at that because I always drank too much) and I wasn't interested in anything other than looking good, being accepted and trying to like myself. It was exhausting. What is the meaning of life?

The only thing that I could think of, and the only thing that gave me peace of mind for a second was writing. I loved writing in school, and I appreciated other people's writing too. Writing is such a window into someone else's imagination and brain, and I wanted to invite people into mine. Throughout my whole life, I had been fighting for people to see me and understand how I felt, but my words couldn't take me there. I thought of what jobs I could have where writing would be involved, and I applied for journalism school the day after.

I studied Journalism at a university in Stockholm over four years. Since I have always liked the structure of having to go to class and having assignments to work on I looked forward to going back to school after a gap year from high school. Excited by my newfound light in the future, I felt a bit of hope. Later I realised that journalism wasn't for me – it wasn't the types of stories I wanted to write and share with the world, but when I applied I thought that Journalism is the only "accepted" form of writing – because you write about real stuff. There were many rights and many wrongs in the school of journalism, and that made me forget why I loved the written word to start with. I soon realised that it is not only in journalism you can write about real stuff.

I wanted my writing to be an emotional compass for a lost person like myself, so that was what I needed to create – I just had to figure out and be open to a way of how first.

Hot Tip

When we feel happy, alive and excited our body produces happy-hormones. It's a natural chemistry. When we think of things that make us happy, we feel happy and our body follows. The more we think of and focus on things that we love, things that excite us and things that we are grateful for, the more of those feel-good chemicals our bodies produce. Gratitude is a good tool to use in order to start seeing the good parts of being alive.

Waking up to a set alarm can be a harsh start to the day, especially if you want nothing more than to sleep a little longer. How we treat this resistance can potentially have a huge effect on the rest of our day. So instead of getting angry about the fact that you "have to" get up, you could see it through the eyes of gratitude. Through the practice of gratitude, you will learn and understand that you don't need to get external satisfaction and constant gratification to feel content. When you depend on constantly getting more and more and more, you let out more happy energy than you take in because you are constantly focusing elsewhere, not in the present moment. Gratitude will help you connect to everything good in your life; here and now.

Action:

I read these wake-up tips in a book called, Three Lessons on How to Lower Stress Naturally, by Angelina and Shane Saunders and they really helped me start my day in the happiest way:

1. When your alarm sings, let your first thoughts be about how comfortable your bed is, how fluffy your pillows are, all the people you love in this world, how amazing sleep actually is (as

supposed to "FUCK, I DON'T WANT TO GET UP").

2. Stay in bed, take 10-20 deep breaths from your stomach and imagine how your breaths wake every cell of your body with oxygen.

3. Think about (or say out loud) three things that you are grateful for today. (Maybe you will get to see all your friends, you might feel extra confident in who you are this morning, you might have bought a new flavour of tea that you are going to try, anything and everything that make you feel excited is a good start to your day).

4. Connect with your body through becoming aware of the fact that it is there. Try to feel yourself in your body and become aware of happy excited vibrations reaching out from your body into the world. (This might take a bit of practice. Chances are that you will have to push it a little in the beginning, but you will know when you feel the connection).

PSYCHOLOGY HOPPING

After Mia and when The Lunch Group session were over, I saw some different psychologists and anger management therapists to help me see my worth, and attempt to figure out what was making me so unhappy. Sometimes my whole family came along to support me; other sessions I sat alone to reveal things about myself that I could only talk about within the walls of the psychologist office. It was relieving in that way, to speak about what was going on inside of me with somebody that didn't know me but tried their best to understand. The man with the twisted moustache, the two ladies, Roland with the ponytail, and last but not least; Sigmund with the anti-depressants.

The anti-depressants, serotonin, helped me to stay alive, but they didn't provide me with passions and purpose – they just numbed all my feelings. I still needed to figure out for myself what life I wanted to live, what I was worth and how you figure all of that out. The antidepressants gave me the strength to start figuring myself out, but it was only a tool to help me tame the storm inside of me. It wasn't even close to a solution but it enabled me to make jokes in the morning instead of fighting with the suffocating anxiety I had got used to living with. The first morning I could actually joke with my dad, look him in the eyes and laugh was a morning of change. It was a big climb towards freedom.

I didn't want to start with anti-depressants but I thought that I had no choice (I always had a choice). I thought that I had tried everything else and nothing worked (I hadn't). If I could go back now I would make sure that, before I even considered anti-depressants; I would have tried two months without gluten, dairy, and refined sugar, caffeine and alcohol. I would limit my food intake to only natural food in its rawest form possible. I would make sure I moved naturally, preferably outside every day. Walking, running, rollerblading, cycling, yoga in the park, anything that makes my blood circulate.

The reason why I wouldn't recommend the jump straight at anti-depressants is because they can make it so much harder to listen to our bodies and learn what they like and what they don't like. It disables our ability to trust in our own capability to help ourselves. Thinking that we need artificial drugs to feel better and to save us might lead us down a path where we start believing that all help is to be found outside of our own bodies and minds. I don't want to live a life where that is the case anymore because it takes away my own power to naturally be the best I can be.

Anti-depressants also come with a variety of side effects that to me are too high of a cost for a quick fix like that.

For people who don't know how serotonin works and think it's like popping happy pills at a night club; it took me two weeks of taking a small dose every day to be able to smile in the morning. Serotonin protected me from falling deep into the anxiety chamber rather than lift me up into a euphoric sky. For some, it can be a numbing medicine, but at that time in my life, I got so high on not getting low. I walked around the streets of Stockholm with my chin up high, with new tools to explore this world with.

In February that year, I was talking to my older friend T. I have looked up to her my whole life, she's a friend of the family, beautiful and secure in herself. She's the reason to why I always wanted to dye my hair red and use lip-gloss. This February day she got angry with me, but mostly at society, when I told her about the psychologists I went to. I told her that they help me to look inside for what is wrong with me, and they tell me that I will be happy when I figure the unhappiness part of my life out. I think that she got angry with me because I kept looking in the wrong places for the source to my unhappiness. She got frustrated because she knew that there is nothing wrong with me as a person – it is the way I look at myself and my role in this world that needed to change!

"I saw red and almost screamed at me never to listen to anybody that tells me to figure out what is wrong with me again, because nothing is fucking wrong with me. It is society that makes us believe that we have to be in a certain way or else we don't belong in it. Or else we are wrong. It is a structural problem. If anything is wrong it is the structure that makes us believe that we are wrong.

Don't ever think that you have to be someone else, or follow norms that you don't agree with, she said. Don't ever try to become more like somebody else or let other people define what is good and bad about you. Once you start to become the most you can be, you'll realise that it is freedom. When you try to fit in this society, you will get angry at yourself, because if you do anything only because someone else tells you to do it and you don't agree; of course you will get mad at yourself. And you will get angry at them for making you do shit you don't want to do. The key is to understand what the structure wants you to do and then question if that is really what you want to do and understand that nobody can make you do anything; you can only make yourself do things. If most people around you are acting in a certain way that you don't feel comfortable with, understand that you can always act in your own way; the way that makes you feel comfortable."

-20 years old

That's the conversation that changed everything because that's when I realised that nobody, not the social structure or any person can make me feel anything. I choose how I feel and if I say that someone else makes me feel a certain way, it's only because I haven't taken responsibility for what I feel and why. When I became aware of emotions that certain people or situations awoke within me, I learnt how to take responsibility for letting those emotions take over. Once I started to understand that people didn't make me feel anything – I feel the way I feel because I am feeling it – not because what other people are doing. As soon as I stopped shifting the blame, feeling sorry for myself for feeling mistreated I could finally break free from being a victim of situations. Once I realised this, I finally felt so much freer in my relationships with people and myself.

Hot Tip

I don't relate to an angry, sad and mean person now, but that was who I was a lot of the time before. It was like I had an alter-ego that took over my mood and energies. The loving, caring, happy and annoyingly excited me got put on the bench just to observe while chaos took place. I believe in food as healing, and I don't think that anti-depressants are the key to every little bump in the road. If I could go back in time, I would teach myself about how food and nutrition can affect my mood.

Happiness, anxiety and sadness are all chemical reactions in our body, and I would provide myself with the best possible fuel to set myself up for happiness and balance. If I could change anything it would be what I put in my body and I would start to take care of my intestines. I truly believe that if I had started to focus on providing my gut-flora with the right nutrition I wouldn't have needed serotonin. A healing and nourishing diet can do miracles for our brain and bodies. If you change your diet and focus on genuine health and nutrition and it's still not enough to motivate a positive change in your thinking then I would only consider serotonin as a kick-start to gain the strength to start changing my eating habits and self-discovery. It would've made me more receptive to the self-love Mia asked me to look for.

Action:

1. Think about a person who brings out feelings of anger, sadness, insecurity or irritation within you. Think about what it is that really makes you feel in that way; is it them and what they are doing or how you are choosing to deal with it? (were you mentally and physically balanced and happy before "they" ruined your mood?)

   a) Is there any way that you can deal with these people that would make you realise what emotions you are walking towards, stop and choose a different feeling.

   b) Can you separate yourself from other people to a point that you feel that they haven't got the power over you or your emotions?

2. Before you make the decision to try anti-depressants, hear the other side out. Kelly

Brogan is a really good and reliable source to hear out before you make any decisions that has to do with adding any form of hormone altering medicine into your routine.

THERE IS NOTHING WRONG WITH ME!!!

For the first time in my life, I understood that nothing good would come from focusing on what is wrong with me. I had to choose between accepting that I am wrong and that the world is unfair and give up trying to ever become happy, or I could take the world for what it is right now and learn from people who are doing well within it.

When I started to look for inspiration in people who were living a life similar to the life I would love to live, I saw that they weren't blaming the world for treating them bad or blaming everything around them for working against them; they were doing what they wanted to do, no matter what obstacles they had to face.

The most important lesson I learnt from T was that people are always going to have an opinion on what you do and how you act, but when you are being you, and doing what you are doing because it feels right all the way inside, those opinions are nothing but just that, opinions.

Now I just had to start focusing on myself. On who I was and how I wanted to express myself. I needed to start thinking about what I loved instead of what I hated and then just do it. I was done with looking for reasons to why living a fun life wouldn't work. To live a fun, happy and peaceful life I just had to do fun things that made me happy and at peace.

The scary thing with shifting focus was seeing my own self-doubt. Without realising it I had struggled with doubts of not being good enough. Doubts about not being worth even feeling that I was good at something. That was for everything, even just being myself. Blaming the world for feeling like I wasn't good enough had masked my reality in which I simply was weighed down by all these doubts.

Self-doubt presented itself in my life as a form of refusing to try things out because I was scared of failing. As soon as I felt a little bit of doubt or resistance I gave up. I didn't dare write and let people read my work because I doubted that what I wrote was good enough, even when I liked it myself. I was afraid of people thinking "who does she think she is talking about this?" or "does she really think that she is good enough at what she is doing to present this?" I doubted that certain people would like me so I avoided speaking with them. I doubted that I could actually live a life that I loved so I didn't dare to try.

I realised that the reason I didn't love my life or myself wasn't because I wasn't worth loving, I didn't deserve it or I was unlucky – it was because I never dared to try to live a life where I could actually be me. That was something I could overcome. That was something I could change. I could dare to try.

Hot Tip

I wish that I had the strength earlier to be myself without constantly worrying if people would be disappointed in me. Every time someone questioned anything I did, I felt this shockwave of guilt in my body. Like my whole world had fallen apart.

"Someone had said that I am wrong and I am not living life right" is what my brain told me. Only that might not have been what they actually were saying. They might have been curious or surprised or testing their own limits. Maybe they weren't criticising me, maybe they were just asking. I wish that I could've just realised that if someone has an opinion about what I am doing it is just their opinion. They are just people too, and nothing they do will give them the right to change who I truly am. If I do things connected to my true values, then nothing anyone says can change the way I act. Don't ever listen to

anyone who is telling you to change if you are being true to who you are. And if they get angry with you about that, remember, it's their choice to get angry.

Action:

1. Think about a time when you disagreed with someone about something, maybe whether something looked good or not, or if a person was fun or not and you felt like you had to believe and feel what the other person thought.

2. Ask yourself, is what the other person believed the truth or just their opinion? Always remember that you are allowed to have your own opinion about everything, and so are they. All people are people just like you! Trust in your own gut feeling, in your own opinion and let others have theirs.

3. Write down three things about yourself that you believe are true. Notice how these beliefs have been holding you back or weighing you down in life.

e.g. I believed that I was the black sheep of my family and this stopped me from feeling like I fit in. I believed that I wasn't creative at all and this stopped me from trying new things or expressing myself. I believed that the only way of loving myself was to look a certain way and this weighed me down because I could never achieve self-love.

4. Ask yourself if these beliefs really true. If the answer to any of them is YES, ask yourself does it have to be true? What can you do to change that belief?

e.g. I am as unique as any of my siblings and I can create whatever I want for myself in my life, changing the way I look will not change the way I feel inside, but if I start listening to my inside and start taking care of myself then I will feel good and then love myself.

5. Next time if you ever feel like there is something wrong with you, remember this: **There is no right or wrong way to be in this world** – there are only people's opinions about right and wrong. You are allowed to feel

everything you feel and be anything you want to be: nobody can ever take that away from you!

You are You
and that is always enough!

6. Are you afraid to dream big because you doubt that you can make it happen? Pretend that the doubt doesn't exist for a minute. Write down three things that you are afraid to dream of? What will it take for you to believe you are worth it?

SECTION 10

SORTING MY SHIT OUT

This section is about figuring out what motivates you and why and then figure out how to do more of that.

THE SPIRAL

Mia always said not to focus on the body and the food; **focus on finding the love for yourself**, free yourself from your demons in your head (through creating space for other things to enter your life) and then the love for your body will come naturally.

I expressed my self-hate and my misunderstandings through my relationship with my body because it's the fastest way to connect with myself, it was everything I knew. Mia created a space for me to think about love. She created a space for me to play with the idea of self-love. She knew that I needed to focus on all the beautiful possibilities in the world rather than the problems I had. In the most delicate way possible she planted seeds of freedom, love and happiness in my brain which had quietly created a dream of one day being free from all of my obsessions.

During my late teens and early twenties, my emotional and physical state went through a circle of stages.

Stage one was driven by an urge to have a healthy looking body. Stage two I got frustrated because my body was taking too long to look "right" so I cut one food group after another out of my diet until fake sugar and nothingness was all that was left.

Stage three was driven by the need to find balance between chaos and restriction. Usually that turned into overeating, panic and vomit.

During all my stages I was equally unhappy. I neglected my real needs and focused on looking healthy rather than actually being healthy. It's only a matter of time until that constellation blows up in your face. I believed that happiness would come when

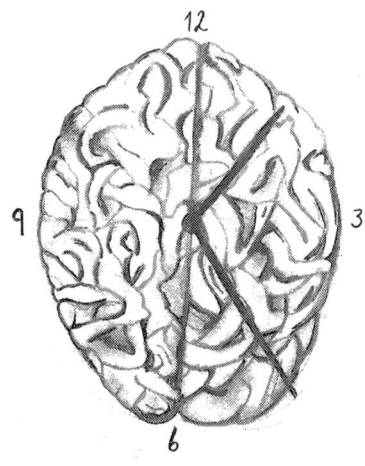

I was happy with how I looked. Now I know that that is not at all how things work, in fact, it is the opposite of how it works. People told me that all the time, but I didn't believe them. I believed that it was true for everyone but myself. I believed that I was the exception. If I could've just used all my energy to actually nourish my body and soul and forget about the look part for a while, I would have realised that **there is nothing more beautiful than a person who is nourished and happy from the inside and out.**

Hot Tip

I have spent so much time thinking about how to change, make up plans for how to become someone I naturally will never be.

I keep wondering what my life would have been like if I had used that time to think about and do things that actually would've made me feel more like myself? I allowed the bullies inside my head haunt me daily, and I just wish that I would've understood earlier that I had the ultimate power to weaken them myself; just by stop wasting time listening to them and open up my mind to a world outside of the world of the mean voices!

Action:

1. Draw a fist sized circle on a piece of paper. Put a dot in the centre of the circle and around the circle write the numbers 0 through to 24 (like a clock that shows all the 24 hours in a day).

2. Draw a line from the 0/24 in to the dot in the middle and out to the 8. Colour that piece in with a blue pen. This represents the time you sleep in a day.

3. You have got around 16 hours every day to think, act and be. With the remaining part of the circle think about how much time you spend thinking about problems, negativity, what you can't do, who doesn't like you, what you don't like. Colour that in with black.

4. The time that is left on the clock represents the time you have left each day. What do you do in that time? Do you explore new hobbies or maybe maintaining something that you like doing? Dance, walk, homework, sing, talk to friends/family, bike, yoga, write?

5. Write down what you think your life would look and feel like if you spent all your time awake thinking about what is wrong with yourself and life. What emotions would be linked to that time?

6. Imagine if you used all your 16 waking hours to think about what is possible, what you love about yourself and the world around you and fill the time with "activities" that make you feel happy and connected to who you feel happy being? What if you used this time to be open to solutions to problems (rather than just think about the problem in itself).

7. Write down, next to the clock, what you think your life would feel like if you spent all waking hours thinking about and doing things that excite you. What emotions would be linked to that time?

THE SOLUTIONS – NOT PROBLEMS

I used to be very quick at giving up and saying that things are impossible. "I can't" or "can you do this for me" were sentences that escaped my mouth daily, effortlessly. If there was something I couldn't figure out how to do straight away I didn't spend much time trying to work it out myself before my frustration of not knowing took over and I gave up. I lived in a world where I was mentally handicapped in the way that I didn't know how to allow myself to grow and become a better version of myself through learning how to handle things – if I didn't know something I didn't know it and I almost refused to learn anything. I was so scared of being someone who has to learn. Instead, I accepted that I couldn't do things, like working out a math problem, draw, dance or learn anything new myself, and because I accepted it I obviously couldn't do it. I had shut down that part of my brain – the resilient part.

As soon as I started to try myself, give every new task a bit of time – accepting that I might not get it to start with but trust that if I give it time I will have learnt something new. If I let myself learn and accept that I cannot know everything I need to know before I have been taught it, life got a little less frustrating and a little more interesting.

I decided that I have to stop giving up so easily. The satisfaction of not giving up as soon as I met a challenge in life was satisfying, to say the least. I started to open up more and more to solutions around me that could help me feel better instead of just accepting that I can't help myself. **I decided that I can help myself.**

Once every couple of months I came across a new thing to add to my weekly routine that could help me feel a bit better, whether it was exercising, figuring out my family tree, cutting down the booze, reading different self-help books, getting to know my hormone cycle and understand how hormones might affect my behaviour and emotions. Each little step helped to build new roads to explore the inside atmosphere of my mind and body and I got a hunger for life.

By focusing on the things I wanted for myself in life I didn't have the time to think of the shit and the mess and the negatives. When my mind was busy thinking about happiness, love and opportunities I felt more of those things and found more of them too. I used to look for the one magic answer to solve my inner pain, but I can now see that there has never been just one solution, even if the root of the issue has been my lack of self-love, trust and faith, no single answer would help get me over that. I needed a whole new view of life, of myself and the society I lived in. Even if no self-help book alone could "fix" my damaged outlook on life, they all contributed with something. They all gave me at least one new tool to use in order to be free, and I don't regret reading and believing in any of them.

I became friends with a girl in my class at uni. She was a little bit younger than me and came from a small town south Sweden. Moving all by herself, to Stockholm, was a big step for her and I felt like she looked up to me a bit, or at least she was curious, because I was such a circus of a human. I was honest with shit that went on inside of me and she wasn't used to having people talk like that. People don't talk as openly about messing up, depression and anxiety, especially when you are brought up in a small town where people all know each other. When I opened up, so did she. There were a couple of her views in life that made me feel anger and frustration. Close-minded and unwelcoming thoughts that she expressed and I didn't like and I couldn't communicate clearly, not without getting frustrated with her for not understanding and feeling the way I felt. We weren't friends for too long but one thing she said really hit home and actually changed my life forever, and for that, I am forever grateful.

One day we were swimming in the local pool and we started talking about life. I saw myself as a very life-experienced person. On an emotional level I suppose I was, but on all other levels in my life, I was still a child. I was 21 years old and lived at home. I had never had a real job, only a few summer gigs here and there. I never had to worry about money because my parents looked after me. My small town friend, who I thought was close minded and didn't know much about 'the real world', had left her home, moved away from her boyfriend and family into a whole new city all by herself. She didn't depend on her parents to spoon-feed her. She said something like, *"what do you really know anyway, you haven't moved away from your family or lived by yourself?"* and it just hit me; I am spoiled. How can I ever learn to live with myself if I keep expecting my parents to clean up all my mess? As I was swimming towards her in the pool I said to her, "You are right, I have to move away from here. I need to learn how to look after myself. I'm moving to Australia for a year". And so I did.

Hot Tip

We can learn something from absolutely everyone. People we like and people we don't like so much. Even though I judged my friend and saw her as close-minded, I realised that on one hand, she was so much more open minded and free than I was. I also learned from listening to other people complain about life that complaining never changes anything. Now, whenever I notice a problem in my life I stop and ask myself, "Now what? What can I do to solve it? Where do I go from here?" I don't always get the answer straight away, but in asking for a solution, I know my brain will start thinking about potential options, rather than just dwelling on the problem itself.

Action:

1. Think about a person you criticise a lot, maybe you don't like the person, maybe it is someone you feel threatened by or someone you feel uncomfortable around. Choose one person and then write down:

    a) Three things that you can learn from that person
    b) Three things that you can learn about yourself by thinking about how that person makes you feel.

e.g. I learned that I could like a person but also hate some things that person stood for.
I listened to what it felt like for her to move away from home to focus on her own future.
She opened up my mind and reality and through her, I could experience what it was like to live with a different mentality

Through her I realised that I wasn't as independent as I believed that I was.

I realised that I can't force another person to feel what I feel just because I believe that what I'm feeling is morally right.

I learnt what it feels like to not be able to get through to another human without changing my own approach to it.

I learned that her narrow-minded thinking annoyed me because I was narrow-minded too, and deep down, I wanted to be more.

Now it's your turn!

MAYA KIUSALAAS

FEELING GOOD

I met Adrian the first day I arrived in Melbourne. My plan was to start my travels in Melbourne and continue up the cost like the rest of the tourists that visit Australia, but destiny had other plans for me, and for that too, I am forever grateful. Adrian and I had no time to play games and pretend that we were too cool to let each other know what we felt. He told me that he dreamed of having pet chickens and that is when I knew, for sure, that he was "the one". Whatever "it" is – he had it. Together we changed because we realised that we wanted to spend time being happy together and there was some work to be done to be able to achieve happiness within ourselves.

We read a lot of books about how to be the happiest, healthiest and wealthiest we could possibly be, and we figured out that if we wanted to create a life for ourselves that would excite us, we had to start dedicating time to live that life now.

Adrian helped me see what I was doing to myself with new eyes. He questioned me, and that made me angry sometimes, but with time that also made me question myself and the choices I made. He planted many seeds in my subconscious that bloomed when I was ready to deal and understand them emotionally. I started questioning if drinking diet soda and adding all these chemicals in my diet was actually good for me (I drank one litre of diet coke per day). I switched from trying to look good and lose weight to feeling good and looking after my body. I cut fake and processed food out of my diet (mostly things that said healthy, sugar-free, diet, slim, fat loss on them), along with alcohol and added natural food and got healthier and happier. I looked better, I had so much more energy, which made me excited to live. Eating for health and life rather than looks brought in a new level of calmness in my life, slowly but surely I stopped obsessing about food, and I started to put all energy into healing my body and my mind.

We started to explore other interests that we have and really put energy towards things that made our souls purr like cats. It took a little while to figure out what it was that we actually liked, but we gave it the time it needed because feeling good soon became addictive.

To this day we keep exploring new ways of maximising our happiness and health, constantly trying new things, always open to advice and change (even if change is scary sometimes). Once again the shifting of the focus has proved to me that anything is possible. I never thought that I could live a life where I actually didn't want to get drunk every weekend, but today I do.

One of my biggest fears, when I stopped drinking every weekend, was that people would think of me and see me as boring. I had an aura of not caring about anything when I used to spend all my weekends drinking and I was afraid that, when I actually started to care about the health of my body and mind, people wouldn't like me anymore. To be honest, a lot of people probably think that about me, because I have changed and in the context of drunken soldiers I am "boring". I have changed a lot. If any of my friends feel like going out to get drunk they probably don't think of calling me anymore. But I am okay with that, because what I have got out of changing that routine is worth everything. I feel good and I am finally interested in life and… myself.

As soon as you start to do something just because other people are doing it or because you think that it's going to make you more beautiful I want to invite you to rethink that. Unlearn what you have learnt and relearn! I want to inspire you to think of health as a resource to connect with the actual needs of your body and mind and from that place, feel amazing.

Hot Tip

*One good thing with setting big happy goals is that you open up your mind for creating your dream life. In goal settings **everything is possible**, and you just have to work with your own soul and imagination. When you hit an obstacle, you will view it as a challenge that you have to overcome in order to move closer towards your goals.*

Every time I feel lost in my life, I sit down with a blank paper, and I picture my dream life in 1-10 years. I try to be as specific as possible but still open for life to take its place. I have a dream house here in Melbourne that I picture myself living and writing in in ten years. For me, that house symbolises the possibility of me being in a position where I can choose to live in that house, but I am open to moving into any house that I can love as much as that house.

It is all about being open to everything life has to offer and see solutions instead of problems.

I am so grateful for my struggles in life. I am so blessed to have had the opportunity to feel so much shit and anxiety, so much desperation and panic because if I hadn't, I wouldn't be able to relate to other people. I wouldn't search all the answers if everything were perfect (or if I was just feeling OK and accept life as it is). I love myself for who I have become through suffering.

Depression has made me connect with love, it has made me see the support around me, and it has made me connect with people through emotions. Through truth. I don't believe that I would've been able to love myself like I do if I didn't hate myself like I did. On the other hand, I wouldn't want anyone to have to go through what I went through. Maybe everybody should feel all the emotions at some point in life, just maybe not for as long, not so destructively. If we all can share how we worked through them, everybody can have the tools to connect with their inner spirit and grow as emotional beings.

Action:

1. Write down 5-10 struggles you have overcome in your life and how they have made you grow as a person.

2. Write down a day in your dream life in 1-10 years (you choose!) What do you do? Who are you with? What do you feel, smell, see touch? Where are

you? What are you working on creating? What are you celebrating?

VISION & GOALS

Through my search for happiness, health and fitness in life I ended up applying for a job at Lululemon in to Melbourne. It is a clothing company but they see themselves as more of a people business where personal development is playing a huge part.

During my first year and a half, I developed a lot. When I wasn't selling stretchy pants, I painted out my ten-year life goals on paper and started to really understand that the possibilities in life are endless. My only limitations are made up in my own brain. The good thing about this company is that they ask you questions about who you are, how you show up, but most importantly; they ask you who you want to be and help you see the possibility of actually being that person.

That year or two I was surrounded by people who all were in their own process of figuring all of this out for themselves. We talked about being who we choose to be, and also how to overcome challenges. Figuring out who you are, who you want to be and where you want to go in your life didn't just happen the first time you sit down to write down your goals. It takes time and practice and flexibility. Sometimes my goals change daily. When figuring all of this out I learnt that this was a process of elimination. I put up new goals, took actions towards getting there, and then as soon as I felt lost again I had to go back and see if moving towards this goal actually made me happier. When it didn't, I found myself a new goal, and suddenly I didn't feel lost anymore.

I felt very safe at Lululemon. Because they helped me figure out my values in life I felt like I had to stay with them forever. I was so grateful for what they had helped me realise; that **I am limitless (and so are you!)**. It is hard to leave something you are grateful for. But I mentally grew in a different way. I found it hard to understand how I was creating love in the world by selling clothes, even though I know that the people of the company are doing so much more than just that. I found it hard to feel authentic when I had to use words like 'luxury' and 'premium' speaking about clothes. To me, it brought me back to high school when my friends and I excluded other people from our group because they didn't feel 'premium' enough.

From creating a future plan, where I saw myself living my dream, fulfilling my passion for writing I thought of starting a blog. But I was scared, the self-doubt kicked in. I got scared of people thinking that I was silly, scared of being judged, scared of making a fool out of myself. I started to write a book, but I felt like the process was too slow. Fuck this, I said to myself, what have I got to be afraid of, and will I let that fear hold me back from trying?

The part of me that cares about what people think shouldn't win and rule the rest of me who wants to do what makes me happy!

Writing gives me pleasure. It is what I love doing, so should my fear of being judged hold me back from doing what I love? I decided no and created my blog; mymondaylove.com the same day.

Hot Tip

When I first started to write down my visions and goals I thought that it had to do with something magical. I thought that by putting it down on paper something will magically happen and it would be true, like a wish. One day I realised that imagining my life in the future is helping me create an inner map of how to act and where to put my focus in order to reach that vision I am creating. Through knowing where you are heading you automatically start to take actions towards getting there. It is helping your inner compass guide you towards the life you want to live. If you don't know where you are heading your inner guidance and intuition will not work as powerfully because it doesn't have anything to aim for.

Action:

1. Picture yourself in 5-10 years. Who is there with you, where are you living, who are your friends, how do your friends act, how do you act, how do you feel in your own body etc?

2. Write down five things you have to do to allow for this to become reality.

e.g. I will have saved up x amount of money to take me on the plane there. I feel happy and healthy so I have been looking after my body and soul regularly, I have nourished my relationship with x and not taken it for granted etc.

3. What are three things you can do today that will bring you one step closer to your vision?

e.g. Start a meditation habit through sitting down and doing it for the first time, call up that friend you see in your vision and invite him/her over to hang out, make a vision board that will remind you of where you are heading every time you see it etc.

GRATITUDE

Gratitude and seeing solutions in challenges rather than frustration in problems have been a huge change for both my relationship with myself and Adrian. Two years after we started to live this life with our new way of looking at things, (reminding each other to stay positive, see things on the bright side, find lessons in mistakes, and learn something new in every hard situation) we look back and realise that it has actually changed our whole life completely.

We don't complain about unnecessary things; we don't accuse each other of not understanding, we don't judge and if we sometimes do; we catch ourselves doing it and use that to figure out what emotion within ourselves that need attention; because we know that a happy, calm person has no need to accuse anyone of anything. If one of us complains about something, the other one asks what he/she is going to do about it. We realise that complaining will get you nowhere other than in a bad state of mind. If the solutions aren't there straight away, we make sure that we are open to receive them and have faith in finding them. Sometimes we sound a bit crazy with all out positivity, but no doubt it has made our relationship so much more exciting, happy, fun and loving. That is a craziness I am proud of.

So many times I just dreamed of winning the lottery so that I didn't have to do anything challenging with my life. I couldn't think of a better life than just having money coming in on a regular basis so that I could just relax, work out, travel and eat. The thought of having a job I had to go to made me feel like the future was too wide and big, and boring. It took me a couple of years of trying, to figure out what I liked and didn't like to do with my time before I could appreciate that struggle and see it for what it was; getting to know myself.

Once I understood that I could either get a job just to pay off my rent and living costs and complain about it or I could dare to try and do something I actually find fun and fulfilling, the choice was easy. Writing has always been in the back of my mind, I have always dreamt about writing books people will enjoy, but I was too scared of putting my writing out there. As soon as I stopped thinking of the reasons why people would like me less as a person or make fun of my writing, I was able to write about what I liked writing about. I felt more and more excited about my future because I realised that it was only my own mind stopping me from trying and doing.

If I won the lottery back then I don't think I would be writing right now because I wouldn't have had to make that choice. Sooner or later I probably would've started to put my thoughts into words, but it would've taken much longer.

I am grateful that I went through the challenges, to stop drinking myself blind every weekend and really push myself to figure out who I want to be. Being so lost in reality, with such a strong need to find my way home, has taught me more about myself than I think would have been possible. That's worth so much more than money. I feel like I am ready for the rest of my life because I have earned all the tools to deal with my reality. I've earned those tools through making all the mistakes I have made, through my willpower to find a way out of feeling like shit and through the love for Adrian, my family, my friendships and myself.

My blog was step one to living the life I choose to live. It was a starting point of me figuring out who I could be, if I just stopped caring about what people thought around me. Being able to openly express my thoughts and battles in life, with everyone who was interested in listening, was such a powerful feeling for me. Sometimes I still feel scared of showing the world the person I am, because I have never allowed myself to be creative before, but the more I write the more I feel that I can understand myself, and that is to me so cool. I grew confident writing about my insecurities and felt proud that I dared to do so. With this new boost of self-fulfilment, I wanted more. I started to listen to Tony Robbins, The Secret, Art Williams, Gretchen Ruby, Wim Hof, Rhonda Patricks, Joe Rogan, Miki Agrawal, Nicole Richie and every inspiring person I could come across.

They all had one thing in common; they believe that we can all do whatever we think we can do. If you want more, you need to believe and do more. I started to see myself achieving great things, which is a cool but also scary feeling. I started to trust my ability to grow. I started to feel that hunger for more. I started to trust that I could do everything I wanted to do if I truly wanted to do it.

The most important thing was to act and not overthink every single thing I did. I acted with my blog. I just started it one day, even though I'm not tech-savvy, even though I don't know anything about making money off a blog. But I now understood that

I don't have to know everything straight away. Me creating a blog that might not look like the most "professional" blog is still getting me one step closer to me running a super successful blog, where I can be a good influence to people who are also trying to get to know themselves. Small actions create big things. Patience, faith, passion and actions have to be the best building ground for any successful project.

Success is a word that scares me a little, in the same way as "luxury" and "premium", but for me, success is to be able to live with passion, feeling as if you are doing good things with your heart and loving every minute of it. I believe that success is the same as happiness, which means that you have to find a balance in life, where you don't just meet one need (e.g. money, health, fitness, social life) but all needs. That makes a successful life.

Hot Tip

The most important question I've ever asked is; If money didn't matter, if I could do anything in this world for a living, what would that be?

As much as I loved the store I worked in, I didn't love the actual retail part of my job. I loved almost every single one of my work colleagues, and I loved the business (most parts of it), but I wasn't fulfilled. If I had enough money, I wouldn't work in a store or for a clothing company.

I would write. I would have a blog, I would write a book, and I would do anything to connect with people through my writing. I would start a podcast or speak on the radio. I would share my struggles in life and be curious about other people's lives. If I had enough money, I would keep writing, talking and sharing. So, that's what I needed to do with my life. I know that now.

Action:

1. Write down what would you do with your time and life if money and rules didn't exist? What makes your soul speak?

    It doesn't have to be specific, like writing, singing or building robots. Do you like asking people questions, biking, organising, debating, reading, the internet?

2. Write down everything that you love doing right now, and just keep doing all of those things until they don't make you smile

anymore. Then you'll find new things in life that will make you happy. Whatever you do with your time, make sure you do it because it makes you feel good or it is a step towards being able to do things that make you feel good.

MAYA KIUSALAAS

SECTION 11

POSTCARD FROM SWEDEN LAND

This section is about questioning if the way you are living and acting is moving you towards the life that you would like to live.

CRAZY IS PERFECT

When I met Adrian, I was in a state of chaos. I was on holidays and drank a lot. I didn't want to work, and I kept asking my dad for money. I just wanted to be free and do what I wanted to do, whatever that was. I will not put words in Adrian's mouth, but from what I understand, he was in a similar position. About to find a "real" corporate job and start entering the "real world" in which you need to wear a tie and a suit and talk in a certain way to fit in. We were both sad to have to start following, the to us, boring rules of how we should act. It wasn't anything we looked forward to, but we believed that that was the only way we could and should go. Adrian had a banking and finance degree, and the "right" move was to go corporate and start "living like an adult".

Adrian and I met and hung on to each other in our now joint chaotic realities. It was like we were each other's tree to hold on to in a wild tornado. We had so much fun together getting to know each other. We lived carelessly and held onto the lives we both had lived before we met. Soon we realised that we needed to change in order to be happy together. We absolutely loved each other, but the destructive lives we were living weren't benefitting our love. We argued about silly things when we were drunk and then we weren't exactly the funniest most energetic people hung over, either. That time of life where you have to take the first step from being careless to taking some kind of responsibility can be quite scary, and we were both just scared to do that. It was scary to us because neither of us knew any way we could live a life we loved whilst working majority of the time with something we aren't truly dedicated to. Instead of stepping into that world we decided to move to Sweden for one year, so that Adrian could live my Swedish life, get to know my family and friends and I could finish my journalism studies. We then planned to move back to Australia and enter the "real" world.

When we moved we had only been together for five months so you can imagine that we learned a lot about each other in Sweden. I would like to say that it was a happy year for us, and in one way it was because we came out so much stronger together on the other side because we had to confront many disagreements at the same times and build a common ground to live on. We realised that we cannot grow together as a couple by telling each other what is wrong with one another. If we want to be together, we need to grow together with love and support. We need to know that we both want to become the best versions of ourselves and then we need to support each other to become that person for ourselves, and for each other and find a way of accepting each other's differences and different processes.

I am fire, and Adrian is air. I am extreme in most things I do, and I carry with me an inner child who can be quite impatient from time to time. Adrian is the opposite, always testing the water safely in areas where I just dive straight in, head first. Through raw communication and openness, we have managed to grow even stronger through the challenges we have been through as a couple. That feeling of knowing that this is my partner forever has been there since we decided to be together, we just knew that we had to find a way to work together for it to actually work out. The more we talk about possibilities to improve, the better our communication skills get.

We both agree that we always have to have an open mind or else we will stagger. The way we have helped each other grow into the people that we are, and want to be, is beyond amazing. Looking back at how we have constantly improved together makes me feel proud, warm and just so full of love for Adrian. Although it wasn't always easy, we did it through our love for one another and that is pretty cool.

For us, our positive journey started like so many other people, I got introduced to the book "The Secret". For you who haven't heard about this book, it is kind of a magical twist on the law of attraction – a little corny but very mind opening if you come from a mental background like mine and are willing to awake your inner child a little.

What you think about becomes your reality. Adrian and I both started to switch our focus from what we didn't want to what we actually wanted. Instead of telling the other person what we didn't want from them we started to let the other person know what we actually loved (and sometimes asked for a change in a non-accusing way; like saying "when I act stressed or seem agitated, try to just give me a long hug and ask me to take a couple of deep breaths instead of just telling me to grow up or get a grip" for example). We started to look for gratitude in what we had. Every night we still ask each other what we are grateful for. Together we read book after book on the law on attraction, positive thinking, health and mindfulness.

The more information we were open to receive, the more possibilities we saw and found in this world.

Did we feel crazy? Yes, we did. But it was a good type of crazy because it actually made us feel closer, calmer and a lot more positive.

2015 was the year we started to create a life in which we both believed that we are already living our dream life; as long as we choose to see it. Time went past, and we got introduced to many more inspiring people, who each taught us something new to add to our life of possibility- Tony Robbins, Wim Hof, Stig Bengmark, Bob Procter, Napoleon Hill, Wallace D. Wattles, Joe Rogan, Nicole Richie, Miki Agrawal, Abraham Hicks etc. We both share this hunger to improve on all levels of our life, constantly. We wanted to learn how to become the healthiest, happiest and wealthiest versions of ourselves. We both love to find new tools to use in life that can help us to improve in one or all of these areas. Together we built a life on faith that we can become the best versions of ourselves, and that we already are the best versions of ourselves at this moment – together and individually, but we can always raise the bar of what is the "best".

Sure, stuff happens that we wish didn't. It's not that we get what we want all the time, but that doesn't mean we quit or stop improving. I used to find all the excuses to why I couldn't do anything. I can't because I am depressed, anxious, lonely, blah, blah, blah.

Whenever anything comes up that is unexpected or difficult or not the plan, we ask, "Now what?", "What can I do, where can I go from here?" If I am struggling Adrian makes sure I see the hidden opportunity and feel the inspiration. He reminds me that life is all about choice and solutions, and I do the same for him when he needs it.

When I was 15 years old I didn't dare to dream about a life I loved as much as I love life now. I just couldn't see myself making any good choices. I dreamed about love more than anything. When I was 15 I felt so overwhelmed with everything I didn't have, that it felt so hard trying to get it all into my life at the same time or even at all. The future felt like such a project because I didn't know any way of seeing anything good in the moment. I only saw the struggle I would have to go through to get "somewhere" in the future. I would have to figure out what I wanted to do with my life, find a partner to share life with and who also want to live the same life as I wanted to live, and of course, at that time I didn't even know what life I wanted to live. I had to find a job that I liked and that meant that I had to apply for many jobs and tell people why they should hire me, something that I found very hard since the only reason I would hire myself for was because I have a fun sense of humour and like after work.

I had got it all wrong, (or I did it all wrong). Instead of thinking about how hard it would be to achieve specific things in the future I needed to think about the small, specific things I could do in the moment to move closer to where I wanted to go in the future. Even if I didn't know exactly where I was heading I had to realise that the future wasn't here now, so the only thing I could do was to do things in the present moment.

It all starts with looking at what you have, what you are, where you want to go and who you want to be rather than what you don't have, who you don't want to be. It's a reoccurring pattern in life.

Focus your mind on what you want, and you will find a way of getting it. You just have to be open for the opportunities, the possibilities and the solutions that are all around you, all the time. So many people have said it before, and I am proud to say that I truly believe in it today; believing has given me the power to act upon it, and I no longer feel like I am the prisoner in my own life, I am always free to choose.

Hot Tip

Something that I have learnt to appreciate is to dream, think big and always be prepared for good things to happen to me. I have been the person who "never win anything" to feel as if I am a person who constantly wins. I see every little win in my life and I make sure I appreciate them a lot. I look for the support I have around me, the people I can count on, the smiles in the world. If someone is rude to me, I don't look for a reason to why that person is being rude to me anymore, I just see someone who needs some love and calm in their life.

Action:

1. Get a jar of some sort, something that you like looking at. Keep it somewhere where you can see it often, on your desk, bedside table, a shelf etc.

2. Use this jar to collect happy memories or dreams.

You choose how you would like to do that. It could be by writing down a dream on a piece of paper and put it in the jar, or maybe put something in that symbolise a memory. There are many ways of doing it. The important thing is that every time you walk past that jar you remember to dream big, to see with love and remember all the good things that life gives you!

MAYA KIUSALAAS

TWO STEPS FORWARD AND ONE STEP BACK

I had to stop and reflect over my situation. I was 25 and the mental progress I had made in my life was quite outstanding. I had gone from living a life where I had no respect for my body or myself, lived with daily anxiety and insecurity to actually enjoying being me. As soon as I started to make choices in my life that supported my new healthy outlook on life and myself; drink less, spend time doing what I love doing, being kind to myself etc. I slowly started to iron out more and more creases of my life.

Because I went from being so careless with myself and my own body, one step closer to feeling great and free might not be the final step in the process, in fact, you can always keep improving. The question is when you are satisfied with the life you live?

Life is a movement and we have to stay aware of how we are moving and if where we are at is supporting our journey towards where we are heading. I swapped out my weekly drinking routine for training and nutrition and for a while I was unaware of how obsessed I got with training. Being obsessed with working out and eating healthy is so much more nourishing than either starving or drinking like crazy, but still, it did affect my life in a way that wasn't really ideal for me. Because training and nutrition had helped me out of a very destructive lifestyle, I felt as if I had to work out hard every day, or else I would lose everything I had gained so far and fall back into my old way of looking at myself (useless, not good enough). I started to believe that skipping a workout would send me straight back to the chaos I used to live in.

On the plane over to Sweden, late June 2016 to visit my family, my head was spinning. How can I not work out for 34 hours and still eat crappy plane food? What about the guilt, how will I handle it up in the air? It was like ants crawling on my body. I felt restless and agitated. I tried to relax, but my head was beating me up with questions. I was so stressed out, I didn't realise it. This had become my normal state of mind. I had put the alarm on 5am to lift weights and do burpees in the back room before we headed off to the airport. I had steamed some broccoli to bring in a Tupperware container and I planned on eating in the car on our way to the airport, to fill up. As we sat down in the car and I cracked open the broccoli feast,

Adrian's mum almost jumped out of the car because of the smell. You never notice that broccoli can smell like boiled eggs sometimes when you steam it in the kitchen? I had to put the lid back on and continue my broccoli feast at the airport.

As soon as I was on the plane I immediately wondered when the food would be served. The next meal was constantly on my mind. I planned what to eat for dinner whilst eating lunch. When, what, how can I eat and still try not to overeat? Every time I went to the toilet on the plane I made sure I did so many squats my thighs and ass burned. I stretched, tried to flex and relax my abs. I was living in a world where I believed that if I didn't work out, I couldn't eat. I would swell up like the sea lion I believed I used to be. It is weird because the more I focus on not eating and maximise my workout – the less content I became with my actual workout and diet. I always felt l wasn't good enough and that I could do more.

We arrived in Sweden in the morning almost two days after our take off. Dad had bought a "summer-car", a Renault Megane scenic, that he proudly came and picked us up in. He said that the guy wanted 4500kr for it, but Dad gathered it up to 5000kr instead. Sweet, I thought. The car was rusty and looked like it had been through… a life before. Sunflower seed shells were lying on the ground from the old owner and his tissues were still stuffed in the side pockets. As Dad proudly pointed it out at the airport car park, we could see it tilting to one side. The back tire was completely flat. There was no way we could do anything with it without a new tire. Dad told Adrian to jump into the car- they were going to find a gas station. Mum and I were left in the car park with the entire luggage and a bottle of water.

When we arrived at the apartment, I needed to work out. I at least needed to do 100 squats, burpees and sit-ups before I could do anything else, my brain demanded it, and I followed – whatever would quiet the critical voices inside of my head. I moved all the tables around so that I could get space to squat. For the rest of the holiday I wanted to put our alarm on 5am, go down to the outdoor gym, meditate for 15 minutes, head back home for breakfast and then start the day. If somebody tried to take that away from me, I felt as if I couldn't breathe. Adrian asked me not to put an alarm on, and I looked at him like he had taken my unborn children away from me. After a couple of days, we started to put the alarm on 7am. That really stressed me out, but I had to compromise.

I thought, "If we get up at 7am we will not be down at the gym until 8am, then we workout until 9am, get home by 10am and have breakfast at 11am. That's way too late"

I felt the stress in my whole body. Every single morning we argued because I got stressed and Adrian got annoyed with me because I was stressing and I was screamed back at him that, "I'M NOT FUCKING STRESSING! ALRIGHT, I JUST WANT TO GO DOWN TO THE GYM NOW! I NEED THIS TO BE HAPPY."

Three weeks in Sweden went so fast. Especially considering that I hadn't been back there for two years. Two days before we were taking off back to Melbourne, Adrian said he had rescheduled our flights and we could stay for another week. He has done many cute things for me, but that's probably the most thoughtful one. I needed to be with my family, and I wouldn't have rescheduled if he'd asked me. I would've stressed over nothing and thought about all my made-up, shoulds and musts back in Melbourne.

As soon as I made fitness and health about feeling good, rather than looks, a lot of things changed in my life. Even though my eating disorders didn't control me anymore, I was still obsessed when it came down to food and exercise in late teens and early twenties. Most of my time I spent either thinking about diets and how to eat to look the way I wanted, or new workouts I could do to get the shape I wanted for my body. When I didn't do that I usually worried about eating too much or working out more.

It took up so much time and I never seemed to get happier. The more I restricted my eating and increased my exercise, the more tired, stressed and almost possessed I became with this urge to look in a certain way. At parties with friends, I couldn't focus on the conversations or be present in the company I was with because my mind was only on food and the thoughts about what that food could do to me. Food, diets and workouts were my life. At the time, I thought I loved it. When I started to look at other things I also wanted in my life I slowly started to reconsider my obsession. I realised that I wanted to be able to just stay in bed some mornings with Adrian, and not have to rush off to get my morning workout done and over with for the day. I wanted to be able to enjoy dinners with friends without constantly looking at the clock – because I needed to get up early to work out again the next morning. I wanted to be able to feel good about doing nothing sometimes, not just because I had earned it through running a half marathon; but because I just knew that my body and mind felt like it.

Life is in constant motion and I had to realise that just because a way of living was "right" for me at one stage of my life – because it saved me from a worse state – doesn't mean that I can't improve it further. I had to realise that I could either settle with this as my way of life, or make another change to my daily/weekly routine to improve life even more. Next step was to handle my obsession with health and workouts and invite a little bit of the unplanned and relaxed life into my life.

Hot Tip

I realised in Sweden, with a click, that I didn't want to be obsessive and never satisfied with the moment. I didn't want to live my life being constantly restricted by my own rules. I realised that I wanted to enjoy every moment, without constantly thinking about what I "needed" to do.

Action:

1. Write down five things that you are doing in your life that you wish that you didn't have to?

e.g. thinking that you have to work out constantly, hold back on food, go to bed early or late, don't walk on any lines on the street, feel anxious when an ambulance drives past, make sure everything is even and balanced everywhere or any routine that you think that you cannot live without.

2. Fight it and try to make your whole being understand that there is nothing that you need to do in order to live the life you want to live. Try to feel that you can be satisfied without doing it. Why not just start living life the way you want to live it now?

3. Choose to live life as it happens, let go of your thoughts of trying to control and manipulate situations. See what happens and be satisfied!

CLICK

Something happened during those extra days I got with my family. One day I just felt this calm in my body. It was like reality punched me in the face with a pillow of dreams, and I realised what I wanted in my life. I didn't want stress, obsession, rules and musts. I didn't want "having to do something" in order to be happy. I wanted to be able to live without always thinking of the next step. I want to be able to have a sleep-in without feeling like I am losing who I am. I want to be able to be on holiday and actually wake up and ask myself what I feel like doing. I wanted to live in the flow of actual life, not in the rules of my own head.

I realised that I have worked out so hard every day for so many years, pushing my body even when I didn't physically felt like it. All those times when my body really would've benefitted from resting; and for what? Einstein said that, *"the definition of insanity is to do the same thing over and over again and expect different results"* and that's what I've been doing for a whole decade. I was a living example of insanity. And I had lied to myself too. I convinced myself that working out made me happy, but the happiness wasn't based on true fulfilment. I had ticked the box, done what my brain has told me I must, to then go out and live my life. When I did it, I wasn't living. Was that the life I wanted to live? A life where something had to be done or else I would feel like shit until I actually did it?

Living by these rules of having to do that every day invited so much stress into my life, and it invited emotions of guilt and dissatisfaction that I didn't need as well. I missed out on so much. I thought it was too late to eat dinner in a restaurant at 7pm, when normal people eat because I would get tired the day after and that would affect my workout. In my twisted head, I thought that eating 'late' would lead to a lost day. The earlier the better for me, and if anyone wanted to do something "after hours", well, bad luck because I was never flexible with my rules. I wanted to go to bed at nine so that I could wake up at five and go to the gym so that I then could live my life. I knew that it's not healthy to work out hard every day. And I know it is not healthy to put so much pressure on myself. Constant mental stress is one of the worst things we can put our bodies through. I would never do this to my child, my best friend or anyone I care about, so why did I feel like I needed to do this to myself?

I cannot tell you what happened in Stockholm those last few days of our holiday because I don't know. I love mysteries, magic and things that we cannot describe with common sense. So I did what every person with a love for the extraordinary do – I turned to the planet movements and Googled what the planets were doing then, in Sweden. My star sign said that it was time for me to decide what life I wanted to live and what values I wanted to have. The planets said that I would come to terms with what is important in life, and without knowing how – I had done just that.

Hot Tip

I used to believe nothing I couldn't see with my own eyes. I took pride in not believing in ghosts or Santa, gods or angels. Not believing protected me from being proved to be naïve. But the more magic and mystery I invited into my life through appreciating when random things happened, the more I saw it. To this day I still don't know how so many things in the universe work, but I do know that life is a lot more exciting to me when I allow myself to have my breath get taken away from me for a moment.

Action:

1. Ask yourself what you would love to believe, if anything in this world could be true? And play with the idea that it might be.

GO WITH THE INNER FLOW

I went to Sweden like a work-out-holic, stressed and with extreme expectations, squatting myself sweaty on the flight to make sure I "deserved" that aeroplane meal. I went back to Australia with no stress in my life and with a calm in my body and mind unlike anything I had ever experienced before.

I started to really feel my body's needs and learned to live in my body instead of in my brain. Did I feel like running or did my brain tell me to run not to get fat? If the answer was the latter of those two, I didn't run. I started to work out only if I felt like it, in my body, and I shut down all the inner-guilt-critics that went off in my head. I noticed that as soon as I let go of my obsessiveness of bedtime, alarm, workout and started to actually find a flow within my body, I entered a new level of calm - a peace of mind that was completely new to me. Weeks went by and the calmer I got, the happier I was with my body and mind. I noticed that I didn't feel bloated, didn't feel lazy or fat anymore. I stopped eating by the clock, and I ate only when I was hungry. I stopped looking up weight loss tips, exercises and slimming program and opened up for the natural way of living. I started to care for my microbiome and my immune system. I stopped eating all these vitamins and supplement I had bought just because I thought they would help me get slim and energised. I basically just stopped stressing and started listening, for real. That was one of the biggest challenges I've overcome in my whole life.

I was free from my rules. Free from my ruler. Free from myself.

Hot Tip

You don't always have to listen to your thoughts you know. ***They are not who you are.*** *Think about it; you can think the most horrible thought or the most amazing ones, you can create things inside your mind that have never happened. You can lie, pretend, explore. But whatever you think doesn't change who you are.* ***You are whatever inside of you that choose what you want to believe.*** *You are the one who can connect it all.*

Action:

1. Put your phone on aeroplane mode and set the timer for 10-15 minutes. Sit down and close your eyes. Breathe from your belly and focus on how the breath travels in through your nose, down to your belly and up to your mind.

2. Try to bring yourself, your consciousness, your awareness into your body and listen to what it is trying to tell you. Don't listen to the thoughts for a moment, just observe them and let go of them by finding the focus of your stream of breath. Feel in your body what you really need, and then, every time you realise that you are living through your head and thoughts – travel down into your body and live in your life's own flow.

SECTION 12

THE END OF THE BEGINNING

This section is about being open to new perspectives, how to get the confidence to do what is making you happy. It is about valuing yourself as highly as any other person in this world; it is about seeing what you have rather than what you don't have.

THE MIND GAMES

Feeling that overwhelming emotion of being stuck in life used to make me panic. What the hell can I do now? When I feel that feeling of having so many things I "have" to do in life I don't know how to do it, or how to find time to do it, I sometimes fell into the pit hole of being a victim of my own reality.

Sometimes I felt satisfied crying over things and feeling a little sorry for myself because I had so many challenges to overcome and right then, I couldn't find the energy to work through them all. The more I thought about how I couldn't get through it all, the more frustrated and helpless I felt. Sometimes in life, it can be challenging to stop ourselves in that frustration and say, "Ok, what CAN I actually do in THIS moment to make all of the things I have got in front of me feel less scary and unachievable?"

Sometimes I have to allow myself to do nothing in those moments and feel a little sorry for myself. Other times I found the strength to choose one challenge to overcome and just focus on completing that. Usually, the satisfaction of getting one challenge out of the way gave me more strength and inspiration to overcome the next, sometimes one challenge is enough.

Our thoughts create new thoughts, like when we bounce ideas off each other (or use each other like ball planks as we say in Sweden) we come up with more ideas that are following the patterns of what we initiated. So when we keep focusing our minds on possibilities, opportunities, love, truth, happiness and health we will figure out ways of growing in those areas, because that's how our minds work. And if we do the opposite, well, you know by now where that can take you.

It has been an exciting journey so far, and the best part of it is that the more beauty and possibilities I see in the world, the more realisations about life and its beauty come to me. Never have I felt more connected to my inner source of life and passions as I am today, just by changing my focus and I am tending to keep going, keep expanding and learn more and more about life and myself every day.

Life is about constantly growing, constantly improving. I understand now, that all the realisations I made when I was younger in my search for happiness, is worth something. One thing isn't going to fix it all, which is what I wanted then. I felt like I had wasted time believing that one thing would fix me. I felt like some of my psychologist appointments had been a waste of time, because they didn't completely fix me. In the moment, when the anger management guy with the moustache, told me to count backwards from 36-0 instead of eating up pages of my mathematics book in anger and frustration, I couldn't see how it helped. I wanted to just be fixed without working on being fixed.

I understand now that they all gave me something, I learnt something about myself and even if it didn't "fix me", they did teach me something and I grew a little, bit by bit into the person I am right now. Sometimes, even learning that some methods don't work for you is a good lesson to have learnt. Today I am so grateful for all the work I have put in in the past. I am grateful for all the shit I've been through mentally, and if I would change anything, I would just be to understand that what I focus on is my reality. That, **I make my life**.

I am proud of my past, grateful for the experiences I have had, for all the lessons I have been taught. I still know where I don't want to go and who I don't want to be, but more importantly; I know who I am, who I want to be, what life I want to live, what people

I want in my life, I know what is important to me now and maybe most importantly; I am excited to learn something new from every situation to constantly improve, because only then can I see how good I can be and how great of a journey life actually is.

Hot Tip

Everything is "impossible" until someone goes out and does it. There are many people throughout history who has changed the status of something that was known to be "impossible". The limits are just in our own minds. The question is, do you care enough about something to make it your mission to make it possible. To bring it to reality?

You might say to yourself, "I can't" even though deep inside you know that you can. Stay with that feeling, Follow it through. Like me, and that silly math problem I had, to me it felt "impossible", and I couldn't find the concentration or the time to solve it, but deep inside I knew that I could learn it if I spent enough time on it – the solution exist.

The same works even with my self-love. Deep inside of me, even when I hated myself and had no idea how to find the love and confidence I needed; I knew that I could, and I knew that it was all inside of me I just couldn't figure out how to access it.

Sometimes it felt hopeless, other days it felt a little easier. The trick is never to tell yourself that you can't or that it is impossible and accept that to be the truth. You have to know that you can do anything you want; you just have to ask yourself: what you want to achieve, accept the time it will take getting to where you need to go and believe with your whole being that you will achieve it.

When you believe in it, in your own ability to achieve anything – you have a purpose!

Action:

1. What is something that you want in your life, that you haven't got at this moment? Something that you really fucking want.

e.g. happiness, contentment, love, confidence, partner, a job, a pet, get into a specific university/school, self-respect, an interest, a passion, a start-up business, abundance, move to Mars – anything!

2. Write down a plan for what it would take for you to get it in your life. If you believe that it

is impossible; there are millions of people out there (past, present and future) who have done and will do the "impossible", look at Elon Musk, Wim Hoff, every athlete out there who ever breaks a record.

3. Take the time to ask these questions
   a) Where do I want to go?
   b) What do I want to achieve?
   c) What do I need to get to there?

Even if you don't know exactly what you need in order to achieve your goal, see if you can grow your trust in your own ability to figure it out. If you can't do it alone; who do you need to contact? Who do you need to talk to? What book can you read?

The most important thing is that you stop focusing on the things that are holding you back in the present moment and start focusing about where you are heading.

Soon enough you will find the faith that you will get there! Just trust in your own ability!

PEOPLE ARE JUST PEOPLE, LIKE YOU

One afternoon Adrian and I headed over to our neighbour's house. They have such a love for gardening and casual art. Their house is like a treasure garden for a curious mind. Fairy lights twinkle in the back yard when the sun gives space to the moon, and beautiful flowers and vegetables live off the nutrition from their worm farm and compost. They are hippies, basically, but they also love partying and wear suits at work. They are people with contrasts and I love that. I love it when people understand that we don't always have to choose one or the other; we can use the best of many worlds. This afternoon the house was full of this beautiful chocolate scent. A friend's Italian grandmother had provided them with the best brownie recipe, and it truly tasted like I was in a chocolate forest made out of Italian love and curiosity.

When we got home later that afternoon, I made soybean pasta with tomato sauce. Cooking has a meditation like element for me. You stir, smell and create something for pleasure. After we had cleaned up, I lay down on the couch next to Adrian and I felt like I suddenly understood everything in the world. I understood what people really meant when they said that they feel like one with a person, Adrian and I share something that only we have together. It was a feeling of 'us' that was all through me for the first time even though I always knew in my mind that I would be with him forever.

Isn't it strange how the smallest moments can hold the biggest answers? We can spend our whole life waiting for a lightning bolt and all it takes is some brownies and pasta!

In that moment I knew it in my whole soul and being. I felt that honesty is everything and that faking who you are is always a tragedy, it's unreal. I could never have this love for myself if I was fake. I could never completely love another person like this either. I got this feeling of life just being a game, and I can actually choose what game I want to play. Even if it felt like it from time to time I understood that nobody actually can make me do anything I don't want to do. Often people would like to think that the life they live comes from the cards they were dealt, but we can always choose to do something differently if we open up our minds to it. I could really feel this strongly in that moment and for a minute it erased all the self-doubts I had of ever being able to live my life in a way I want to live it.

I realised that it is all a game, everything is a game, and I can make up my own rules. I can actually choose what game I am going to play, and I am going to master the game I want to play because I am going to love it, with passion.

The most revolutionary realisation I had that night was that, I am a person, I know what I want, and no one can take that from me. No one knows what is best for me and I don't actually need anyone's approval in life. I realised that I actually don't care about what my boss, old friends or random people on the streets think of me, because if they don't understand the things that are really important to me, in my life, then I don't need their opinion, and that is okay, it doesn't mean that I don't like them or that we cannot be friends still. I only want to do things that are coming from me with joy and excitement, and I felt that night that I actually could choose to live a life where I do just that. **I just have to listen in and express whatever is going on inside of me.**

I know that to achieve my goals and dreams, I need to preserve this confidence and bring it with me wherever I go. And when I meet people out in the world who act in a way that makes me feel as if they are trying to put me down, I need to use my confidence to see that it actually has nothing to do with me. Nobody can make me feel anything unless I allow them to. I have to distance myself from letting people have that effect on me and take responsibility for my own projections. That means that instead of blaming others for making me feel less of a person, angry or sad, I have to realise that I am making myself feel that way, because I allow people to have that power over me.

Hot Tip

I wish I knew before what freedom meant to me. I was always looking for freedom from my self-made prison and I was looking in all the wrong places. Now I see freedom as following your emotions, working with what excites you and what you are passionate about. It is a beautiful place to live.

When you know that you do what you do out of love and for freedom; don't ever listen to anyone telling you to change and behave on his or her terms.

Action:

1. How are you expressing your true self? Write down one, two or three ways you can connect to yourself.

    Do you have a way of connecting to that person you would be if nobody else existed, a way of communicating with yourself? It can be through words, paintings, conversations with others, reading, listening, dancing, sewing, swimming, riding... anything that makes you feel like you are doing what you are doing only for you.

2. Write down three things that you think are holding you back from doing the above-mentioned things on out of fear to "stand out" or to look "stupid" in front of others?

3. Is there anything you wish that you could do but you are too afraid of what other people might think? Write it down.

4. Do one thing today that gets you out of your comfort zone.

e.g. Say, 'Hi' to someone you want to say hi to, say, 'I'm sorry,' to someone you have hurt without making excuses, smile on the street when you are walking alone or whistle on a song, sit with new people in school, start a conversation with a person you haven't spoken to, ask for help.

MAGIC

Ever since I was a little child, I have loved the thought of magic actually existing. I love everything that makes me question what I know is true, and I love stories like Harry Potter that make me wish for a place like Hogwarts to be real and that expand my own imagination. On that note, I bought a couple of crystals on the medieval week on Gotland, an island outside of Stockholm. I must have been around seven years old and to me, they felt magical. I looked at them and wished for them to take me along for a journey.

When I moved back to Australia with Adrian, after we had spent that year in Sweden, I brought my stones, alongside a few new ones I had bought. The man in the store had pointed out two stones to me; a red and a blue one and told me to get them together because if I kept one in the left and the other in the right pocket it would make me feel like a princess. I thought, I've always wanted to feel like I can do whatever I want, so I bought them and carried them around with me.

Over the next six months, I added a couple of new stones to my collection. I love playing with them and wishing for them to bring strength, calm and magic into my life. If it works even as a placebo thing it still works, right, so why fight it? I figured that life gets more exciting if I play with the thought of magic, so I will allow myself to be a little crazy as long as it is fun.

A girl in one of the stone shops told me that I should cleanse them and charge them with new energy under the next full moon, so a couple of days later I put all my stones down in a bowl of water and set them out in the moonlight for a cleanse. I changed the water and left them to charge in the sunlight the following day.

Two nights later I was sitting on the couch writing words of wisdom down on a piece of paper when I glanced over and saw my stones resting on the window frame. A thought struck me. How many stones do I have? I counted and saw nine stones in different shapes and colours, including one super small one I found somewhere on the street. What about the planets? How many planets are there? Eight planets, excluding Pluto. I stared at my computer screen showcasing the planets in colour and order.

One by one I could connect the stones to a specific planet. They were the absolute perfect colours and size to match them and I even had a giant see-through Jupiter. I Googled all the stones and amazingly; they each represented one of the planets. I felt like… the whole universe had opened up to me. The stones had seriously taken me for that journey I once had asked for and it really felt like magic, I mean it is quite crazy isn't it?

It even turned out that the two stones, the red and blue one that I had to buy together, are Mars and Uranus. Mars is the ruler of the Aries, which is my star sign, and Uranus is ruling Aquarius - Adrian's sign. I started to connect more and more of these dots and it just made me feel so curious of what I don't know yet, and that is a really good feeling to have.

Hot Tip

The more I started to play with the idea that I could make anything in this world possible if I just started to believe and open up to it, the more optimistic I got. I shifted what my mind allowed me to believe was possible. I took more actions that I ever would have dreamed was possible before having the solar system in my pocket. Instead of treating life as unjust and insecure, I started to believe that things would go my way – I could make them go my way through not giving up, through valuing what I had. Through understanding the gifts I collect are much, much bigger than I could have possibly imagined and they all fit together so perfectly. And even if I don't know that straight away, I will be shown with time.

Action:

1. What is the highest belief you have of yourself and your world that is your life: what do you want and believe that you can achieve?

2. What would be even higher than that? What don't you dare to believe (yet)?

THE END, THE BEGINNING, WHATEVER YOU WANT IT TO BE

Hopefully, by now, you have realised some places in your life where you have been lost without even realizing it. Hopefully, you have learnt how to know when you are being you, and when you are trying to be someone else.

Life is like a walk in the forest. If you don't pay attention to the path you are walking you will get lost. In the same way, you will lose yourself if you don't pay attention to how things feel in the present. Being confident in who you are is all about knowing why you are doing things you do. It's about making conscious choices to do more of what make you feel strong, that get you to place you want to go. To be the very best **you** you can be, do more of what makes you feel at home.

I want you to **make yourself a promise** that you will keep trying to connect to your true self. Go back and re-do all or some of the exercises whenever you feel lost or unmotivated and you will find that your answers will change constantly; because who we are changes all the time. Change can be scary, but scary is good too, because it means that we are living. And even if you choose not to change, know that everything around you will always be changing and growing and giving you suggestions for how to move on.

Hot Tip

What I have learnt about life that has made me feel happy, content, excited, full of love and beautiful from the inside and out is:

1. *Listening to what I need and who I want to be, and then choosing to be that person in that exact moment has given me confidence.*

2. *Being around people who make me feel good and who question "things that just are" gives me life.*

3. *Taking care of my body and mind because I want to feel good (rather than looking good) is the way to feel happy and content. I stay open to new things; don't get too stuck in my routines. I want to keep an open mind to invite improvement into my life constantly. My way*

isn't always the best way so sometimes I have to challenge my pride and my ego in order to grow.

4. *When I feel stressed, I have to break down why I feel stressed. Most of the time I realise that I don't have to be stressed I just think that I need to. I meditate and ask my body (not my brain) what it needs to find peace.*

   Wim Hof said, "Don't take life too seriously, it is serious enough as it is".

   When I stress out over nothing or feel as if I am not being good enough I remind myself of that, I remember that love and happiness is all that matters in each moment.

5. *Listening to my emotions and understanding where they come from allows me to actually get to know myself. I can now accept emotions without panicking.*

6. *I live the life and that I want to live now because I don't want to waste any time doing shit that I don't like. Life is about growing, and I want to grow in a*

direction of possibility and like every part of the journey.

7. *Be open-minded. Try new things, walk new paths, meet new people and ask questions you want to know the answer to. That's how I grow, that's how I expand my life, and that's how I get rich on experiences. I am sometimes too comfortable with what I do and I forget (or avoid) putting myself in new situations. Sometimes new scares me, and I work myself up and get anxious to start something new. I need to give myself a push in the right direction and remind myself that I will not learn new life skills if I don't try new things.*

8. *Seek out the truth in everything you care about. The truth is that there is a truth, but that truth can change from person to person and from time to time. If I always try to do what is true to me here and now, and always be open to explore the land of truth, connecting to the source of truth, then I will feel like I am, and I will be on the right path in life.*

9. *I love meeting happy, funny, open minded, excited, loving and curious people, so I choose to be one*

myself. I treat other people with love and honesty. I know that they are human, like me, with their own emotions and thoughts and fears. If somebody says something, it doesn't mean that that is the truth. I now feel, and trust what I feel.

10. *I don't limit myself to what I think that I can be. I dream big and make it happen. I am aware of the fact that there are always actions I can take to move towards my biggest dreams. Once I understood that these were actions everyone has access to, I truly felt that I can take charge of my own reality.*

11. *Seeing what I have now is my way of being present and happy in the moment while building on my dream for the future. I appreciate where I am, what I have, and always choose who I want to be in this world. I make sure that I learn in every moment and feel happy and grateful for how far I have come.*

The minute I stopped looking at what I didn't have and who I didn't want to be a whole new world of possibility opened up in front of me.
Try it.

12. *Mute my ego. As soon as I realised that I don't have to make everyone understand or believe that I am right and they are wrong about something, as soon as I started to accept that people don't have to believe what I believe or see what I see, as soon as I stopped trying to convince everyone to see and do things my way I grew stronger than ever.*

The amount of energy I have wasted on being in conflict over nothing just to keep my pride is crazy. I have stopped spoiling my ego and I feel more peaceful than ever doing so.

Action:

Remember to ask yourself as often as possible:

1. Does following this trend, or unwritten rule, make me feel like I am connected to my true self?

2. Am I doing this out of love for myself or to change who I am to fit in?

The key to winning any fight is to find love for whoever you are fighting with, no matter if that is your sibling, friend or yourself.

No matter what the outcome of the fight is, when you love them you win. They win. It's a great strategy. If love is too big of an emotion to embrace in the moment; use gratitude as your guidance and soon enough you will love.

Every time you are frustrated with another person, yourself or a situation, stop and remember three things you have got to be grateful for with the person, yourself or the situation.

Choose to start a good spiral towards freedom by focusing on feeling free. What's the first thing to be grateful for? (That they are here with enough passion and love for you that they want to argue their point and for you to understand.) What a gift.

FOLLOW THE TRACE, BACK TO THE SOURCE…

Below is a list of some people who can offer further information, inspiration and expertise. Start looking through their content and see what speaks to you at this time of your life.

You can always find more up to date inspiration and sources on my blog; www.mymondaylove.com I have collected a list of all the books, podcasts and videos that I gained inspiration from. I will always keep my eyes peeled and ears pricked, ready to learn more.

Before you do that though, here is a list of people who been major contributors in their different fields and who all have helped me unfold my life piece by piece, and who have all been a great inspiration in my writing of this book:

Physical and Mental Health & Nutrition:

Dr. Rhonda Patrick: foundmyfitness.com/

Kelly Brogan, holistic psychiatrist, neurobiologist & a lot more: kellybroganmd.com

Giulia Enders, scientist – *GUT – The Inside Story of Our Body's Most Under-rated Organ*

Chris Kresser, Holistic health: www.chriskresser.com/

Motivation and Action:

Tony Robbins, motivational speaker: www.tonyrobbins.com/

Miki Agrawal, entrepreneur and inspiratory: www.mikiagrawal.com/

Brené Brown, researcher & storyteller: **www.brenebrown.com/**

Steven Pressfield, author, *The War of Art*

Jordan Petersson, clinical psychologist, cultural critic and professor of psychology - https://jordanbpeterson.com/

Gretchen Rubin – *The Happiness Project* and more great books on happiness.

Rhonda Byrne – *The Secret*

Eckhart Tolle – *The Power of Now: A Guide to Spiritual Enlightenment*, Spiritual teacher - **https://www.eckharttolle.com/**

TRY IT OUT!

Here is a list of things to try out and see if it wakes something up inside of you, something that you might like:

Write down five new things you will start to do daily that will make you feel a little bit better each day, like: add a green vegetable, smile at yourself the first time you see yourself in the mirror each day, say three good things about yourself before you get out of bed, say three good things to another person, take ten deep breaths and find an inner calm before you start your day etc.

- Express your emotions through painting and drawing
- Just paint/draw whatever comes to mind
- Speak in front of an audience (there are Toastmasters clubs out there for people who would like to get into public speaking)
- Dance – take a dance course, learn from the internet or just shake your limbs, however you do it, make sure you feel alive
- Yoga
- Learn about pickling vegetables and the benefits it has to the human body
- Get a 1000 piece puzzle and make it
- Design clothes/redesign clothes you have already got
- Swim
- Call a friend you haven't talked to in a while

- Write a letter to someone you miss
- Start/keep a diary
- Start a dream journal
- Make a collage
- Make a vision board
- Ask if you can visit a workplace you are interested in
- Look up and see if the libraries in your area are putting on something interesting like a book club or a writing course
- Learn how to cook or bake
- Make a recipe book with all your favourite dishes in it
- Try a new sport: Boxing, Sprints, Crossfit, Yoga, Pilates, Circus, Riding, Martial Arts, Karate, self-defence, Gymnastics, Dancing, Soccer, Footy, Hockey, Tennis, Squash, Volleyball, Netball, Ice skating etc.
- Read a book

- Plan a trip (even if you are not ready to go on one right now it is sometimes fun to just create a dream trip that you will go on in the future, when you are ready)
- Watch stand up comedy
- Learn a new language
- Take some photos or do a Photography course
- Dress up
- Make a film
- Pretend that you hired yourself to clean your own home/room – how homely can you make it?

Now it's your turn…

MAYA KIUSALAAS

ALL THE THANKS!!!!!!!!!

I am filled with a lot of gratitude to all the people who have encouraged me to keep working on this book when I sometimes doubted if I am actually the right person to shine light on these self-destructive subjects. Today, thanks to all of you, I know that I am, because I feel so much for everything I share in this book, and I truly wish that it will end up in the hands of those who feel a lot, and those who know people who feel. A lot.

THANK YOU ♥Adrian who I have accused of not believing in my capability of actually finishing something (which I realised when writing this, is just my own fear of not being capable, and my own self doubt projected). Thank you for pushing me to create something that inspires and feels good, even though my story is quite heavy.

Thanks to my brothers for letting me share our story, through my experience and to use your documentation.

Thank you Mum for providing me with so many emotional drawings (some I heard you drew balling your eyes out) and being able to stay positive, never blaming me for treating you like shit and holding my behaviour against me – because you always knew that I had, and always will, have endless love for you.

Amber Weller & Zandra Zbinden for thoroughly going through and helping me see things with a new, educated perspective.

Anthony Ross for helping me realize how shit the book once was, which made me step up and not just lazily reject it, like I normally do - before I had actually put in the hard work of editing it properly!

Temi Katonis, Tali Morgan, Isabel Westrup & Ellika Fenno for reading this in it's early stages and give me some really good feedback and confidence to the story.

I have to give **my biggest thank** to someone I have never met in person but who has taught me so much about the art of writing and composing a book; Honey Reither, who I would've never gotten in contact with if it wasn't for beautiful, wonderful and supportive Josephine Tang. Thank you too for helping me see and feel the value of my book and believing that it will truly help all the lost souls out there! Sometimes I almost think that you don't live on this earth....

I also feel as if I should thank my dad for something too ...for just raising a thunderstorm child without letting it get to him (almost at all).

Made in the USA
Lexington, KY
13 November 2018